THE LADY LINCOLN
SCANDAL

THE LADY LINCOLN
SCANDAL

VIRGINIA SURTEES

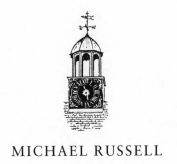

MICHAEL RUSSELL

First published 1977
as *A Beckford Inheritance*

This edition published 2000
by Michael Russell (Publishing) Ltd
Wilby Hall, Wilby, Norwich NR16 2JP

Typeset in Sabon by Waveney Typesetters
Wymondham, Norfolk
Printed and bound in Great Britain
by Biddles Ltd, Guildford and King's Lynn

ISBN 0 85955 260 8

SASHA
'... and wave beyond the stars that all is well'

Contents

	ACKNOWLEDGEMENTS	ix
1	*Background to a Farce*	1
2	*Paternal Solicitude*	10
3	*Marriage and a Love-letter*	23
4	*'I Shall Live for You'*	36
5	*Anglesea Ville*	53
6	*Lady Lincoln and Lord Walpole*	71
7	*Mr Gladstone's Mission*	89
8	*Discovery and Flight*	101
9	*The Earl of Lincoln's Divorce*	113
10	*The Farce Played Out*	125
	REFERENCE NOTES	137
	INDEX	139

Acknowledgements

To Her Majesty the Queen for gracious permission to quote from Queen Victoria's Journal, and passages of her letters published in *Dearest Child*, and *Dearest Mama*, for which she holds the copyright.

The Duke of Newcastle has most kindly given me unrestricted permission to quote from the Newcastle Papers deposited at The University of Nottingham, where Mrs A. Welch, Keeper of Manuscripts, and the staff of the department, have given me every assistance. With my indebtedness to the Duke of Newcastle, I wish to add my thanks to the Estate Accountant, Mr A. E. Pacey.

I acknowledge with thanks the permission generously given to me by the Duke of Hamilton to draw upon the Hamilton Papers, at Lennoxlove. At West Registrar House, Edinburgh, Miss Doreen Hunter facilitated my study of the material, for which I thank her.

For leave to make use of the Gladstone, and Newcastle, Manuscripts at St Deiniol's Library, Hawarden, and at the British Museum, and to quote from *The Gladstone Diaries*, I am under great obligation to Sir William Gladstone, Bt; in this context I wish to thank Mr Geoffrey Veysey, County Archivist, Hawarden, Flintshire. To the Earl of Harrowby I owe a very special debt of thanks for much kindness, and to the Harrowby MSS Trust for latitude in the use of the Harrowby Papers; I am also beholden to Miss Main Macdonald, lately archivist at Sandon Hall. My thanks are due to the Marquess of Londonderry for allowing me access to the Londonderry Papers at Durham County Archives with permission to quote from them, and to Mr J. Keith Bishop, County Archivist, for making them available; to the Earl of Harewood for leave to quote from Lady Canning's Papers, Leeds City Archives; and to Viscount Cobham to quote from material in his possession; also for access to papers from Knebworth deposited with Hertfordshire County Council. The Abbé Alphonse Chapeau has done me the exceptional kindness of allowing me to read certain unpublished letters, once thought to have been destroyed, from Cardinal (then Archdeacon) Manning, and to quote from them. Without the records of the proceedings, and the evidence given on the Second Reading, of the Earl of Lincoln's Divorce Bill of 1850, which have contributed the keystone to this tragicomedy, this sketch could not have been attempted, and I thank the Clerk of the Records, House of Lords, for having allowed me to consult and make use of the information derived from them.

For having guided me to Lady Lincoln's grave, I should like to thank the Reverend F. A. Thompson, and for other acts of particular kindness I am grateful to the Hon. Betty Askwith for reading my manuscript and making suggestions, Miss M. Fraser-Gamble, Mrs Jean Gilliland, Mr Roger Hudson, Miss Jane Langton, Registrar of the Royal Archives, the Reverend Prebendary Harold Loasby, Miss Mary Lutyens, Mr Keith Miller Jones, Miss Sophia Ryde, Mr John Saumarez Smith, Signora Giovanna degli Uberti. I have consulted, and been helped by Mr Wilfrid Blunt, Mrs Cohn Davy, Dr J. C. Corson, Mr Brian Fothergill, Mr P. L. Gwynn-Jones, Mr O. Wyndham Hewett, Dr Rosalind Marshall, Mrs Henry Nevile, Mr Guy Nevill, Dott. Ing. Ippolito S. Parravicini, Miss Y. G. Parrott, Mrs S. R. Pepper, Major Herbert Turnor.

I thank the following for permission to quote from published sources: Oxford University Press (*The Gladstone Diaries*); Constable and Co. Ltd (*Mrs Gladstone*); Evans Brothers Ltd (*Dearest Child*, and *Dearest Mama*); John Murray (Publishers) Ltd (*My Dear Duchess*).

Marks of omission have not been introduced in quotations, except in particular cases. Original spelling has been preserved.

I

Background to a Farce

On the last day of January, 1837, the 4th Duke of Newcastle, writing in his library at Clumber Park, made an entry in his diary, 'A heavy and most grievous affliction has fallen upon us. I forbear mentioning what it is any farther than that it concerns me as a parent in a manner least expected of anything that could happen to me.'*

The tragicomical incident which so oppressed His Grace was the discovery, through the interception of a letter, of a clandestine flirtation being carried on under the Duke's own roof, between Susan Lincoln, wife of the Earl of Lincoln, the Duke's son and heir, and her brother-in-law, the Duke's fourth son, Lord William Pelham-Clinton.

The weeks before Christmas had passed slowly and perhaps a shade lugubriously for Suzie, for her father-in-law could in no way be termed a convivial man. A widower† at an early age, and ill prepared by his own solitary and singularly unhappy childhood, he had dutifully brought up a family of ten children for whom he felt a strong and possessive affection, though little understanding. To his four daughters and six sons he was an intimidating figure, exacting a total subservience to his views, which in Parliamentary and Church affairs were narrow and bigoted, and which at home in the monotony of family life were no less uncompromising. His probity, his honour, his adherence to duty, were never in question, but any innovation in private or public affairs earned an unflinching disapproval. In 1831 his castle at Nottingham, situated on an eminence dominating the town, was burned by a mob provoked by his opposition to the Reform Bill; the memorable speech in which he referred to his ejection of some Newark tenants ('Is it not lawful for me to do what I please with my own?') has passed into the annals of this country's history. But notwithstanding this prejudiced outlook, when he

---

* Newcastle Papers. Subsequently denoted by ⁿ.
† His wife, Georgiana Elizabeth, daughter and heiress of Edward Miller Mundy, had died in 1822 in childbirth.

looked inwards the Duke bore himself with humility. His was an honest faith (if staunchly Tory Church of England), and throughout his diaries he unburdened himself to his Creator, offering up a broken and a contrite heart to the service of Almighty God. At Christmas and Easter the members of the family who knelt at the altar to take the Sacrament were counted and written down; the scholastic attainments of his children were noted with scrupulous care; and over the years he recorded with devastating exactitude the casual mishaps and minor illnesses, such as prevailed in any family. But to the Duke nothing was casual, everything bore the imprint of potential calamity, particularly where his family was concerned; for here indeed was his treasure. His pride and trust in his sons, his hopes for them, were unbounded. 'Dear noble fellow' he frequently wrote, and as one by one they failed to match up to his aspirations, he found, in some alien influence, explanation for the loss of filial obedience.

Parliament drew him regularly to London: bringing with him his four daughters, he would take up residence at the town house on the north side of Portman Square, which in consequence of having been built on high ground was thought to be particularly salubrious, thus recommending itself greatly to the Duke who was seldom free from a general despondency regarding the health of his family. In 1820 he had entered upon a ninety-nine year lease of No. 17, still one of the most beautiful of London houses, and then of fairly recent construction, having been built by Robert Adam in 1776. The pedimented porch and severely ordered brick façade, with roundels and panels of swags placed at regular intervals between the sash windows, would have attracted the passer-by but would have given little suggestion of the elegance of the interior.* When the family of eleven was at full strength, there must have been some doubling-up; for though the upper floors contained a series of pleasant apartments, the ground and first floors were given up to formality, if so portentous a term could be given to these faultless rooms. Their disposition, the variety of their varying shapes, the designs in stucco, the motives, lunettes and medallions, the painted panels, the grisailles, all executed under Adam's inventive genius, seemed to vie with each other

---

* Renumbered in 1859, it is now No. 20. It was occupied by the Courtauld Institute of Art, but since the removal of the Institute it has become a club.

in offering a ravishing display of the architect's creative powers. But something more than the perfection of the curving staircase and the distinction of the rooms was required to call them into life; yet gaiety, diversion, dash, were hardly to be expected of the Duke. Of these dissipations his children (the girls in particular) had really no experience. The Ladies Georgiana, Charlotte, Caroline and Henrietta Pelham-Clinton were painfully shy and enjoyed little in the way of society since their father was always on the look-out for a slight, whether purposely or unconsciously administered. With his affairs in London completed, the Duke, accompanied by his daughters, would return to the oppressive silence of Clumber.

Yet despite his many idiosyncrasies this diehard Tory, noble in bearing and of unassailable rectitude, was in many ways a lovable man, and at Clumber and Worksop, his Nottinghamshire estates to which he devoted his wealth and time, he was seen to advantage. Worksop had been purchased in 1837 from the Duke of Norfolk for £37,000, while the domain of Clumber, more woodland than park, linked in legend to the days of Robin Hood, had been carved from a portion of Sherwood Forest and stretched back in history to close on a thousand years. Clumber, famous for its beech and oak and long avenue of limes, extended its prerogative for some eleven miles in circumference. Here towards the end of the eighteenth century, fronting a lake covering two hundred acres, was raised the white classical house, from stone quarried on the estate. The state drawing-room, the crimson, the yellow drawing-rooms, the white marble hall said to be unsurpassed in England, the great dining-room with its magnificent plaster ceiling, the chimneypieces of signal beauty, in particular that of the smoking-room from Fonthill Abbey, the French furniture, the chandeliers, all pointed to a discriminating and eclectic taste. The Duke had acquired statuary for his central hall from Nollekens's sale in 1823, and in the same year, buying from the Fonthill Abbey sale, had enriched his collection of pictures; to these, in 1848, he added paintings from the Duke of Buckingham's dispersal sale at Stowe. From Hafod, the Duke's Welsh property near Aberystwyth which he sold in 1845, twelve years after its purchase, he removed the fine collection of books to Clumber. But while he spent excessively on the embellishment of his houses, his recklessness in adding to his estates was inexhaustible. In two years he was said to have spent half a million pounds on buying property; but there he was seen at his happiest, out of doors amongst his tenantry, riding his horse about his estates and supervising the running of them.

The heir to these possessions was Henry Pelham Fiennes Pelham-Clinton, 12th Earl of Lincoln, born in 1811. The first time he spent a night away from home was when he went to Eton at the age of thirteen. His tutor, Mr Thompson, a valued friend and adviser of later years, found him industrious, courageous and modest, qualities instilled by his father's upbringing; he seems also to have been surprisingly well-equipped for the rough and tumble of school life. Possibly his association with nine brothers and sisters had eased his path, though there can never have been much rough and tumble to brag of at Clumber. With William Gladstone, eighteen months his senior and at Eton at the same time, he was as yet not very intimate, but when in 1830 he went up to Christ Church, Oxford, the friendship ripened, and although close ties were formed with Charles Canning, Henry Manning, De Tabley, Sidney Herbert, H. G. Liddell (later Dean of the college), with none was he so closely linked as with Gladstone. This was a life-long friendship. Together they had come under Tractarian influences; the Union Debating Society, of which each had been President, served as a platform for their political future. No stauncher friend supported Lincoln through the bitter days of his middle years, willing even to face the witness box in defence of his friend in the shattering scandal of divorce.

Though not a scholar and lacking the brilliance of some of his contemporaries, Lincoln was a tireless and conscientious worker, ambitious, high-minded, seriously inclined, awake to his responsibilities, and if never an inspired speaker yet able to expound with conviction and energy. Moreover, in early manhood his frank and affectionate nature was not yet concealed behind a mask of reserve, and in 1831 at the age of twenty, when his father after prolonged deliberation was writing to the Duke of Hamilton on a matter of vital concern to his son and heir, he presented an appearance altogether pleasing. Tall above the average, a figure well-proportioned, dark expressive eyes lending charm to an otherwise serious countenance, the streak of priggishness later to bedevil his relations with his wife not yet apparent, he seemed to carry within him all the attributes to attract a young and impressionable girl. But for one exception: the saving gift of humour was not within his grasp.

At Eton and again as a young man at Oxford, Lincoln numbered among his friends the Marquess of Douglas and Clydesdale, only son of the 10th Duke of Hamilton and Brandon. Though of the same age their tastes for the most part lay in contrary directions, Lord Douglas's at this time leading no further than the enjoyment of a pretty girl and the dissipations of the Turf, while Lincoln's were those of a politician in embryo; but their shared enthusiasm for sport assured Lincoln a welcome to shoot in Scotland on Hamilton preserves, and among Lincoln's earliest surviving letters is one addressed to his father in 1830, desiring a Clumber spaniel for Lord Douglas's use.[n]

These visits to Hamilton Palace in Lanarkshire, twelve miles from Glasgow, and Brodick Castle on the Isle of Arran, must have had a quite extraordinary effect on one brought up in a Tory stronghold in which a rigid code of behaviour prevailed and where display was censured, for his host was a man who in almost every particular was the direct antithesis of the Duke of Newcastle. A Whig, a rake, an avowed Bonapartist – his obsession with Princess Pauline Borghese, after seven years' marriage to a young wife, had scandalized society – opulent, though preserved from vulgarity by a consummate taste, highly cultivated, eccentric in dress* and often absurd in manner, tolerant of the ways of the world, but dominated by an overweening pride of his ancient lineage, Alexander, 10th Duke of Hamilton and 7th Duke of Brandon, premier peer of Scotland, claimed the Scottish throne as his birthright and the French dukedom of Châtelherault, dating back to the sixteenth century, as his heritage. He had enjoyed a spirited youth and middle age. Before succeeding to the dukedom in 1819 he had been elected a Member of Parliament for Lancaster for four years at the beginning of the century, followed by a mission to St Petersburg as Ambassador where he had invited notoriety by a love affair with the once beautiful Countess Sophia Potocka,† by now an 'old battered beauty'.[2] On his return to England, where his financial demands had already prolonged negotiations for five years, he married in 1810, at the age of forty-two, Susan Euphemia, the

---

* Even when old, he held himself as straight as a grenadier. 'Never was such a magnifico. He was always dressed in a military lace undressed coat, tights and hessian boots.'[1]

† She had been a slave, born near Constantinople in 1761. Bought, married to a Colonel de Witt, divorced, and remarried to Count Felix Stanislas Potocki, patriot, and one of the richest noblemen of Poland, she had only recently been widowed.

twenty-four-year-old daughter of William Beckford of Fonthill
Abbey, author of *Vathek,* to whom, through her mother Lady Margaret Gordon, daughter of the 4th Earl of Aboyne, he was distantly
related. With her he secured an immense fortune, both by the marriage settlement and as eventual heiress to her father's wealth. Of this
union a son was born the following year. Shortly after the birth of a
daughter in 1814 he visited Napoleon on Elba, and from about that
time dated his infatuation for Pauline Borghese. He was in Italy with
his family, full of rheumatism and seemingly advanced in years, while
the Princess, still bewitching though ravaged by illness, was nearing
the end of her spectacular career. She spoke of him as assisting at her
toilettes in the mornings, handing the hairpins to her dresser, 'faisant
métier de bouffon malgré ses rhumatismes'.[3] But the burlesque was
brought to a timely conclusion by the death of the 9th Duke in 1819,
when his son was obliged to return to Scotland. His fair enchantress
did not forget him and at her death bequeathed him a silver-gilt
dressing-set, and to his wife a pair of Sèvres vases of great beauty. His
little girl, Suzie, or Toosey as the child mispronounced her own
name, was the recipient of a ring set with opals.[4]

What, one might venture to wonder, were the sentiments of the
Duchess at the irregularity of her married life?

Her own childhood and upbringing had been exceptional, for her
birth at La Tour de Pelz, near Vevey, in 1786 had precipitated the
death a few days later of her mother, leaving her elder sister Margaret
and herself in the care of their Beckford grandmother and a succession of Calvinist governesses. With their grandmother's death they
passed under the supervision of a cousin, Lady Anne Hamilton, sister
of the future Duke, and lady-in-waiting to Caroline, Princess of
Wales. By 1802 the 'Pledges of Love', as they were collectively
known, were installed in a house in Fonthill Park, for Beckford, despite his passionate homosexual indulgences, had been a devoted husband, even if his moodiness and prodigious vanity made him a
temperamentally uncertain father. He had a variety of names for his
daughters: Susan was 'the Hysteric'; Margaret, 'the Egoist' who had
been disinherited on making a runaway marriage in 1811 with a
despised Colonel Orde, had earned herself the further sobriquet of
'Mrs Ordure'. Peace was scarcely restored before her death seven
years later. Colonel Orde's deficiency appears to have been caused by
three of his immediate family having taken holy orders.

With the splendours of the Gothic abbey of Fonthill as a drop-curtain to girlhood and the influence of a corrupt and fanatically extravagant parent as a guide to the comedy of life, there was yet much to gain, for William Beckford was after all a man whose artistic taste and knowledge were second to none, and whose rare books, paintings, jewels, carpets and furniture, collected with monomaniacal fever, were recognized throughout Europe.

In addition to her many accomplishments, Susan, the younger daughter, displayed a transcendent charm and a very particular beauty (both of which later captivated the Duke of Newcastle) which, together with her father's wealth, made her an enviable match and ensured her a host of suitors. Beckford had endeavoured to force her into marriage with a homosexual friend of his own, the Spanish Count of Egmont, and when this failed the unseemly bargaining for a ducal coronet began, terminating in marriage and a munificent dowry. The Duchess seems to have maintained a harmonious relationship with her elderly husband; they lived a great deal abroad, in France and Italy, and they had perfect command of both tongues. Their letters to each other, as well as their children's, were written in French – the language, too, in which they carried on conversation among themselves, for the Duke, it will be remembered, claimed the Dukedom of Châtelherault, and was at pains to get his title recognized. His pretensions led him, when in Paris in 1825, to exert his prerogative by demanding the *petites entrées* at Court, thus causing the Duc de Damas (groom of the Bedchamber) to call aloud, to the astonishment of the pages: 'Laissez entrer le Duc de Châtelherault.' The Duchess too had presumed to ask for the privilege of a *tabouret*.* 'Madame, vous voilà à votre place!' exclaimed Charles X of France. Both these incidents disposed the Duke of Hamilton to assume his claim to have been acknowledged, but Lady Granville, the British Ambassadress, noted that when pressed, 'that perfidious monarch, Charles X, entirely denies that he has admitted the claim or given any decision on the case, and when reminded of his speech to the Duchess, he said that any English Duchess who asked for the *tabouret* should have it equally with those of France. This was the unkindest cut of all, since it robs the barren honour of the only distinction it conferred.'[5]

---

* 'Avoir le tabouret', the distinction afforded to a duchess, allowing her to be seated, on a stool without arms, in the presence of the King.

From her letters and from glimpses of her through the eyes of others, the Duchess emerges as a woman of intelligence, perfectly aware of her irresistible charm, and though responsive, yet so forced in manner, and her true worth of character so overlaid with sentiment, that one might be led to suspect it of artifice. It is more likely that her expressions of excessive affection, which indeed were adopted by the four members of this mutually admiring family, were the result of the society in which she had grown up, and of those – mostly foreigners – amongst whom she now moved. Later, her daughter Suzie Lincoln, of no like intelligence, persisted in protesting her affection in a yet more exaggerated manner, reflecting in her letters to her father his own almost passionate devotion to an only daughter. A suggestion of the effect which the Duchess was apt to make comes from the not wholly unprejudiced pen of Lady Granville, writing from Paris in 1825. 'The Duchess of Hamilton looks thin, but always beautiful. Her manner I think very disagreeable, so forced in gaiety, making her so little available as a companion on any subject. All my natural thoughts and movements abandon me when I am sitting with her, and I remain looking at her fine face, now all astonishment, and now all animation, and now all tenderness for the Duke, just as I sit looking at a diorama.'[6]

It was against this background that Lady Susan Harriet Catherine Hamilton grew up, an adoring and cherished child, petted and spoilt from infancy, who had inherited much of her mother's charm. Her attraction, often commented upon, seemed to depend as much upon her irrepressible spirits as upon the beauty of her very fair complexion and chestnut hair and dark wide-set eyes, while the parted lips, suggestive of slightly protruding teeth, seem in no way to have detracted from her good looks. Accustomed to being the centre of attention, to being praised and admired, her nature, at once happy and irresponsible, sparkled in the sunshine of her parents' loving indulgence. To have her own way she had learnt early to dissimulate, though this, and a tendency to selfishness, went unperceived since all things were hers for the asking. At home at Hamilton Palace, a fairy-tale palace of splendour and riches, her formal education had been attended to. In 1825, when eleven years old, she was taking lessons on the pianoforte in Edinburgh for three months, for the sum of £9. 16s.; also Italian lessons from a Signor Bugni for the same period, amounting to one pound less. Her dancing lessons stood at £8. 15s., while her dentist's bill was cheap at three guineas. Judging by her ill-formed handwriting, and her subsequent inability to pay her bills, it is not surprising to find her at the age of fourteen still having instruction in 'Writing and Arithmetic' to the tune of two guineas for twenty-four lessons. The harp, that most requisite of all attainments, to which she applied herself in 1827, was, at the price of £20 for two months, the most costly of all. Abroad, her manners and general comportment gained elegance and polish, she learnt the ways of society, and perhaps also not to lay too great an emphasis on marital fidelity. Writing of his grandchildren a few years earlier, William Beckford could confidently say: 'The children, with their accomplishments and lively grace, are so lovely, prepossessing, vivacious, and Roman, that they attract and delight every glance.'[7] To be thus appraised was very agreeable to Suzie, for to be flattered and petted, the focus and consideration of many, well suited her disposition; nevertheless her beguiling charm earned her for many years – even when most highly tried – the loyalty of friends attracted by her lovable nature. That her affections were volatile, and her need for admiration unbounded, were not yet apparent.

2

Paternal Solicitude

While Suzie was putting up her hair, trying on her new ball gowns, *
and dancing her way into society, the Duke of Newcastle was passing
through a melancholic period. He was forty-seven, ten years a widower, and in conformity with his usual attitude, at odds with the
political climate of the time. He had ten children on his hands; his
estates were encumbered by debts through his extravagance; worst
of all, his health was profoundly disturbing him. 'My health suddenly gave way', he wrote, 'in consequence of the long continued &
intense strain upon it, & as the attack was a sort of complication of
maladies, of an intermittent character with several concomitants, I
am left in a very shattered state. I am assured there is nothing consti-
tutionally wrong, so that I shall yet hope to see brighter days.'[n]
A brighter dawn was breaking. Fortunately for him the Duke
could not see through what dark night and blaze of scandal the
morning star would lead him. He was preoccupied at this time with
parental responsibilities, regarding it as his duty as a father to find a
husband for Lady Georgiana, his eldest child, now nearing twenty-
two; or for her sister, Lady Charlotte, two years her junior. (The two
younger were still in the school-room.) Since his daughters rarely
went anywhere or saw anyone it was unlikely that they would attract
suitors of their own; besides, anything so progressive reflected an
infringement of convention, and was therefore deprecated. On
November 21st, 1831, after weighty deliberation, he wrote the following letter† from Clumber to the Duke of Hamilton, marking it
'Most private & confidential'.

> My Lord Duke, It has more than once appeared to me that your
> Grace's feelings & mine may probably coincide upon a subject
> which deeply interests us both. For myself, I can truly state, that

---

* At that period the word 'dress' was used only by ladies' maids.
† Hamilton Papers. Subsequently denoted by [h].

the subject is one of most distressing anxiety to me, on account of
the very peculiar situation in which I am placed with regard to the
females of my family, which makes it of the greatest importance
for the others, as well as for themselves, that my eldest daughters
should be desirably settled in life.

I will not disguise from your Grace that there is no young man
in the country to whose charge I should so readily & confidently
commit the happiness of my daughter as Lord Douglas. From my
son's unexceptional & remarkably high character of Ld Douglas,
both for principle & conduct, & from what I have had the pleasure of seeing, I am so much encouraged to give full credit to what
I have heard of him, that you may suppose how much joy it would
give me, if I could see that prospect realised which, in my view of
it, might be productive of those mutual advantages which I anticipate.

I must throw myself upon your Grace's goodness to pardon
what may appear to you to be an extraordinary step on my part; I
would not however, attempt to give encouragement to what I so
anxiously desire, unless it met with your Grace's entire approbation. It is not Ld Douglas's situation & eminent prospects, but his
high character which prompts me to covet such an alliance. Feeling assured that he is qualified duly to estimate the value of
females (such as it is my pride to own that my daughters are) pos-
sessed of all those mental & personal endowments which are capable of making an honourable husband happy.

I shall forbear from entering farther upon this subject until I am
made acquainted with your Grace's opinion. I have only to entreat
your favourable interpretation of this strictly confidential communication upon a subject of such extreme delicacy – & to have the
honor of remaining your Grace's

faithful & obedt servt   NEWCASTLE

The Duke of Hamilton was nearing sixty-four, by seventeen years
the Duke of Newcastle's senior, but his reply,[h] written from Hamilton
Palace on November 27th, reveals a sprightlier temper as well as a
more lively pen. It reveals also a more calculating eye.

It is most true, there is a sympathy of feeling between us. I am
proud of it. Those very feelings that have induced your Grace to
write to me distinguishing Douglas in the most flattering manner

in which a parent could distinguish any young man, were operating upon my mind at the very same moment in regard to Lord Lincoln; & when your letter arrived, strange as the coincidence may appear I had almost resolved, with equally good reasons, & upon a similar conviction to address your Grace in a similar strain.

I have an only daughter, the object of my tender affection & most anxious solicitude, & the proposal I had in contemplation to make was of the same nature with the one which I have just been honoured with from your Grace in so handsome a manner.

Permit me to say that Ld Lincoln is already well known here through the medium of my son, and because known, he is esteemed and beloved. I rejoice to find that your Grace participates in such sentiments as may tend to unite our families, if such a union is congenial to any of our children, as (I frankly confess) it would be gratifying to me.

But having said thus much I must subjoin that the realisation of such projects I consider as beyond my reach, & partly out of my province, for whatever parents may desire they cannot, ought not, to command although they may endeavour to direct. In so delicate a point as one that embraces the whole course of domestique life, I hold that must be left to the spontaneous feelings of the parties concerned. All the parties in question are young, perhaps too young to decide for themselves or to allow us at this moment to look to any immediate decision. I shall rejoice in bringing them together under the hope that the wishes of the parents may be confirmed by the partialities of their children.

Both Dukes had a son and heir to be caught in marriage, but as a bride Susan was ostensibly the better catch, as being an only daughter she would bring a larger dowry than any one of the Pelham-Clinton girls could muster. Lord Douglas on the other hand with his handsome looks and his reputation as a fine dancer might, in the dazzle of his eventual inheritance, be excused a somewhat defective temper and a sad aptitude for imprudent extravagance. But he would be reaching his majority in two months and was unwilling to compromise his emancipation by the cramping bonds of marriage; also very probably his father had schemes for a more impressive alliance, for though the Duke of Newcastle's overture had been acknowledged

in general terms, no direct consent crowned the specific proposal –
but it drew a counter-proposal from Hamilton Palace.

At Clumber the receipt of this letter was electrifying; it gave the
Duke 'a new life & cheered my spirits which have been painfully
shattered by a sort of general *unhinging*'; it not only opened to him
brighter prospects for the future ('if', as he added with his usual tendency to despondency, he was spared to 'live to witness them'), but it
also presented the pleasurable necessity for a very long letter[h] in
return.

> Your Grace has only proposed to me what I would gladly accept.
> I presume that Lady Susan is all that may be looked for from a
> daughter of the Duchess of Hamilton – & that character, temper,
> & every female virtue have been deeply cultivated, that happiness
> from such an union must be next to certain. It has already been
> my wish that Lincoln should turn his attention towards Lady
> Susan Hamilton & observe whether she would meet his view of
> what he would look for in a wife. Should this prove to be the case
> on acquaintance I think I can take upon me to engage that
> Lincoln would most readily be led by my advice, & I am much
> mistaken, if he has not already a feeling of interest towards Lady
> Susan. I know not whether he has ever spoken to her, but I am
> quite sure that he is by no means insensible to her appearance. It
> was my intention more than once to have spoken to him upon the
> subject. I meant to have asked him whether he gave a preference
> to Lady Susan Hamilton. I think I know what his answer would
> be.
> When I have inculcated & incited him in the observance of
> purity of morals I have always held out to him the prospect of
> early marriage – so that I am persuaded that his mind is made up
> to that course. It may seem strange, but his virtuous principle is so
> strong, that I had no doubt when he was last with me that vice had
> not stained his mind. I can add with real pride & thankfulness that
> of ten children all are delightful, & truly excellent, so that anyone
> who entered my family circle would not go into bad company. As
> yet my family is so little known that I mention this for your satis-
> faction.

A reply was awaited with suspense, each day adding to doubt and
surmise, till at last 'my heartfelt satisfaction therefore on receiving

your truly kind letter yesterday was very great, & eased my mind (just now in a most uncomfortable & sensitive state)'. The Duke of Hamilton had counselled moderation and an independent choice for the participants in the proposed courtship. 'I entirely concur in all your Grace's opinions,' the Duke of Newcastle acknowledged, 'I have seen so much misery resulting from forced marriages & so much mischief done by officious interference on the part of the Parents, that I would not for any consideration place myself in that situation. It is however perfectly legitimate to lead without appearing to do so, & to manage the matter in such a measure as to let it seem to be one of individual choice.'[h]

The pattern of courtship had been planned by correspondence: it now required the actors to enter upon the stage. Lincoln at Christ Church was 'at present fagging hard, being ambitious to take a first class'. With the Christmas vacation came the opportunity for a thorough interrogation. The result, news of which went directly to Hamilton Palace, was most satisfactory. 'He has the strongest inclination towards Lady Susan & would be most happy to cultivate the acquaintance, which I learn from him is already formed between them. The consummation of our wishes therefore rests with the Lady, if she does not object on a farther acquaintance, "c'est une affaire finie". I can only add with regard to my son, that my admiration of him is even greatly increased, his excellence & perfection cannot be exceeded, they may be equalled' (a hasty acknowledgement of Lord Douglas's perfections) 'but I can safely say they cannot be surpassed – & this I assert after a very accurate observation & impartial scrutiny.'[h] Lincoln had shown uneasiness at a rumour that Suzie was to be engaged to the Marquess of Abercorn, but his father had been able to 'allay his apprehensions. He has evidently fixed his hopes of comfort & happiness upon an alliance with Lady Susan. He thinks her manner perfect, gay & cheerful, but not forward, & possessing that sort of conversation which is agreeable to his notions.'[h]

On the evening of May 1st, three weeks before 'my admirable Lincoln's' twenty-first birthday, matters advanced in a conventional fashion. Lord Lincoln, at 17 Portman Square, stepped a few paces to the east with his father and two elder sisters, and drank tea at No. 12, the Hamiltons' town house. It was only a family party and a kind of breaking in. On returning home that night the Duke of Newcastle admitted in his diary that he liked Susan extremely, and the Duchess he considered 'a very superior person evidently'.

Lincoln returned to Oxford a few days later. Political life had attracted him since youth and there had never been any doubt where his ambition lay, but during that Trinity term academic work absorbed his energies, so that when a candidate was needed for Newark, one of his father's Parliamentary constituencies, Lincoln suggested his friend William Gladstone for nomination. He wrote: 'I have now known him for several years and feel convinced that his honest unflinching integrity of character combined with talents far above the common stamp, even of those who are called clever men, will be at once an ornament to, I fear, a most *unornamental* House, and an honor to the patron who shall introduce him. He always was both here & at Eton so strict with regard to religion &c as to incur from some a charge of *sanctity*; but as this term implies to my mind in its usual acception *hypocrisy*, I never could perceive any thing of the sort in him. I believe him to be most perfectly orthodox, and in short think that when you stated what he *should* be you only drew a picture of what he is.'[n] There was to be little vacation that summer for Lincoln; after outstaying his prescribed holiday at the Duchess's express desire, to attend the ball for Douglas in early July in Portman Square, he hastened to resume his studies and reading for his degree, and the very next day settled at Cuddesdon in company with Charles Canning, for the remainder of the summer. Being now aware that the attachment between himself and Suzie was reciprocal, he wrote immediately to his father authorizing him to speak to the Duchess on his behalf ('Say any thing, for whatever you may say will fall short of my thoughts and my affection'), at the same time qualifying his sorrow at the sudden death of his pony, in the knowledge that it had died at the very time that 'Lady Susan and I were finishing our country dance' in Portman Square. On her side Suzie made three rapturous entries in her pocketbook: 'July 10th Our ball. July 11th *He* left us. July 13th I wrote to him.'[n]

The Duke lost no time in calling at No. 12. 'I saw the Duchess & Ly Susan & found the latter fully prepared to give her consent & her whole heart to my dear & admirable L & thus that point is settled.' The mission was concluded with perhaps unpropitious celerity. The Duke however was fortunate in recognizing in Suzie every perfection and accomplishment. 'I should do her the greatest injustice', he wrote in his diary, 'if I did not own that her behaviour has been as perfect a thing as I can imagine, from a warm hearted, open, generous, amiable & most engaging girl. She is not less good than beautiful.' As the summer progressed he wrote again: 'The more I see of Ly S the more I like & admire. She is not a common person, & possesses a mind & devotion capable of anything – full of talent, spirit, & energy, but yet tempered by the most feminine graces – beautiful in face & figure, without affectation, the picture of good humour & happiness.'[n] His good opinion extended too to Suzie's parents. He was captivated by the Duchess of Hamilton, and seemingly disarmed by the Duke's kindness, and had probably never before witnessed such conspicuous affection as the family displayed amongst themselves. 'The Duchess of Hamilton is a most extraordinary woman,' he confided to his diary. 'The handsomest & most perfect woman in appearance that I ever saw, with a dignity & pervading grace & elegance which must be seen to be understood.' Her singing he found to be superior to that of a professional, so too her science and execution in music. Her devotion to her children was repaid by 'unbounden affection – it is an edifying sight to see her & the watchful attention of the other, waiting as it were upon every turn of her mother's countenance'. Her conversation was all that might be expected, a 'soul & elevation of mind that excites reflection'; in short 'all that she does, says or thinks is marked by superiority.'[n] As the daughter had captured the son by her ingenuousness, so the mother had consciously fascinated the father by her charm. Nor could the Duke find any fault with Suzie's reply to Lincoln's proposal by proxy. 'My ambition [she wrote] – and may I make use of the word – my duty henceforth will be to prove myself worthy of obtaining the name of your child. I shall make *use* of all my *influence* and encourage *our* dear Lincoln's studies. I shall urge him on to these.'

Arrangements were made for the Hamiltons to come to Clumber in August. Lincoln was working ten hours a day at Cuddesdon and his father saw no necessity for these studies to be interrupted. Not so the Duchess or her daughter who were at Bath with William Beckford. Susan, emboldened by the 'perfect confidence in *your* goodness', was the first to plead for the sight of her lover for two or three days at Clumber, but in terms calculated to irritate by their exaggeration, and because till now the Duke had been the sole arbiter of Lincoln's movements. 'I throw myself upon your mercy before I begin,' she wrote. 'Oh my dear dear Duke, imagine with what feelings I must connect my first view with that most interesting place', and though 'the candour of my nature may make me indiscreet', yet she acknowledged that his decision would be the right one. 'I glory in the thoughts of having a right to claim your opinion as a command. With an anxious heart and trembling hand', she remained, 'with filial devotion, Your very affecte & dutiful Susan.' A blunt refusal followed this reasonable request, whereupon the Duchess, wielding her pen on behalf of a daughter who she felt had earned a little indulgence, herself tried what flattery and tact might do. 'Well my dear Duke, like a *good* father you have refused Suzie's petition, & I like a *bad* Mother differ in opinion from you. I am not at all surprised at your Spartan courage, it is what I have been accustomed to from my beloved husband who no doubt thinks you are *quite right*, but tho' I admire your heroism I cannot imitate it.'[11]

The Duchess and Suzie arrived a few days later – that the Duchess was only 'tolerably well' found a careful entry in the Clumber diary, and a peep into its pages within a day or two reveals how, in spite of his strong prejudice, the Duke of Newcastle was obliged to yield to feminine importunities. 'Aug. 25. I have been grievously annoyed & deeply mortified by the point which the Duchess & Ly Susan have made of seeing Lincoln here.' But, the Duchess having been rendered quite ill, there was nothing for it but to comply, while considering it a great deal of nonsense. Susan again had recourse to *Peacock's Polite Repository or Pocket Companion* 'Ornamented with Elegant Engravings', and chronicled on August 29th: '*He* arrived at Clumber.'

The Duke of Hamilton had been the first to arrive, travelling by night ('I always wander by the light of the moon'), and though it smacked of the irregular his host found him 'so kind & cordial that it is a pleasure & true satisfaction to have him with us'. This pleasure must have been intensified in the shared delight of cultivated tastes and superior knowledge of art. Preliminaries to financial settlements discussed by the two fathers augured well. It was a pleasurable surprise to the Duke of Newcastle to learn that Suzie had considerable expectations of her own, for his own estates were so weighted by debt that the utmost he could do for Lincoln was to allow him £3,000 a year. These matters absorbed both Dukes for the next months, but with contrasting attitudes: Newcastle, perhaps unwillingly forced to recognize and bring into the open the extent of his financial mismanagement, was almost morbidly slow at reaching a decision, and the Duke of Hamilton, generous, helpful, buoyantly accommodating, was eager for Mr Brown, his man of business, to travel south and complete matters so that the marriage might take place in Scotland in November.

The party at Clumber dispersed, the ladies in the direction of Leamington from whence came a graceful note from the Duchess for the return, per coach, of her forgotten 'eternal spectacles', and, while praising the Spa waters, attributing the improvement of health and 'irritable nerves' to her sojourn at Clumber – quite in conformity with her host's observation that she was the better for Nottingham air. A hint obtrudes, well smothered in maternal affection, that hers was the firmer will and more prudent mind as regarded her daughter's material welfare. 'You could not confer a greater favor upon me than by letting me go hand in hand with you in arranging the preliminaries of an union which I trust will be productive of much happiness. I am so persuaded of the superiority of *your* judgement, and I may truly say that Susan feels it to be equally her duty & her inclination to study to please you.'[n] Aware of the parental discipline by which Lincoln's life had so far been ordered, a 'Mother about to entrust him with her dearest treasure upon Earth' thought it well advised to introduce an argument for their living on their own. 'I continue to lay a great stress on the young couple having a *Home*.' She proposed Ashton Hall, their house in Lancashire which, uninhabited and lying half-way between Clumber and Scotland, might be a welcome suggestion. 'You know me well enough now to rely on the sincerity with which I say that I think young married couples should be left to themselves. I would never interfere in Susan's domestic concerns. Her husband is the person to whom she must look up for advice & *to him alone*. Her tastes, her character must be formed *by him*. These are my notions of a woman's duty.' The delicate skill with which she negotiated the tricky matter of a dress allowance – customarily provided by the husband – was worthy of a doughty strategist. 'You are as usual most kind, my dear Duke, & in reply to your query about the 500£ pin-money, I can only say that if it could be 600 you would I am sure settle it so', though conceding, with sufficiently wifely submission to satisfy her correspondent, that 'the Duke understands business so much better than I do that I am always anxious to refer any point to his decision'.[n]

Suzie, learning from her mother of the transactions being made on her behalf, wrote to the Duke of Newcastle, judging him 'too kind and I must say too *just*, not to agree with my dear Mamina about our having a home of our own, at the same time let me assure you that you may rely upon *my* doing everything to prevent our establishment from incurring any unnecessary expense. My whole attention shall be given to furthering the interest and welfare of my beloved husband, and to please *you*, our dear Father.'[n] The Duke could not but have been touched by the fervour with which she emphasised that her 'greatest, I might almost add only, wish now and hereafter must be to do what is most agreeable to you'.

Shortly after this his interest was greatly roused by dire news concerning Suzie. Health, always a trump card with the Duke, engaged all his sympathy, and the first intimations from Leamington of spasms, fits of fainting lasting all of eight hours, the application of leeches, inflammation, pain, nerves 'most dreadfully affected', were sufficient to waken all his compassion. But these afflictions were only the prelude to illness which was to take possession of Suzie's frame of a kind bearing all the symptoms of a true hysteric, and which collectively and before very long constituted a familiar pattern, becoming almost a habit of life and, in its severest form, resulting in paralysis, loss of sight and memory, bringing her to the threshold of death. Had the large family party at Clumber been a subconscious revelation that she would no longer be the one idolized daughter, and that delicate health would be the sure means of regaining the centre of the stage?

At present its effect was to bring Lincoln hurrying to her side, and Suzie scribbled down in the last days of September: '*He* came to Leamington.' 'My face very painful so had leeches put on – very unwell.' 'Very ill.' 'Still poorly.' '*He* left Leamington.' She was quite well enough a few days later to address her 'bien aimé Papino' in response to sound advice he had sent her, perhaps with foreknowledge, or at least suspicion, of her volatile disposition. It made her tremble, she wrote, when she considered that the happiness of another – and *such* another – would be her responsibility. That her future father-in-law should expect her to be an example to all young married women was a delightful notion, and she assured her father that she realized how much her future happiness must depend upon her own conduct, but with parents like hers to watch over her

'autant mariée, qu'auparavent' – she was confident that she could
not go astray. (This reluctance to detach herself from doting parents
to whom she could have constant recourse and who could be relied
upon for partisanship in her endless self-pityings and vindications,
partly doomed the marriage.) From these high-flown sentiments,
more commendable had they not been so short-lived in practice,
Suzie unexpectedly showed her mettle by enquiring whether the
Duke of Newcastle had seen to the recovery and reentailing of the
estates, for though he spoke of marriage settlements he was in no
position to make them without first providing for them.

Lincoln's departure from Leamington was bound up in his can-
vassing the Tory seat of South Nottinghamshire, for with his marriage now a reality the temptation to achieve his Parliamentary
ambition forced him towards an immediate political career. He was
prepared to sacrifice the likelihood of an honours degree and content
himself with a Pass. Thus he and Gladstone would be standing for
seats in the same county. From Holyrood House the Scottish Duke
wrote his apologies to Clumber for having mistakenly carried away
Lady Georgiana's gloves, and, to 'calm her ire', sent a present of
game from Arran. But concern for Lincoln's progress was uppermost
and another note followed at once; signing himself with one or other
of his customary valedictory flourishes: 'Adieu – believe me to be
with regard and affection, My dear Duke, your truly attached &
faithfully yours H & B', he added a postscript, blithely (if irrele-
vantly) expressed in French: 'Je pars pour Hamilton demain', unconsciously calculated to irritate its recipient who held in abhorrence all
foreign practices. He was again writing in encouraging terms from
Hamilton. '*Vile Whig* as I am, you must be sure I feel an anxious
interest. Pray inform me how matters are going on: & if you would
allow me to add it I should like to know how Mr Gladstone was
received; for I have two papers, and in the one all is most generous,
& in the other urbanity & politeness totally abandoned.' When
reports of Lincoln's eloquence reached him, he wrote to congratulate
'and rejoice as much as a Vile Whig can rejoice at the success of Lincoln. My creed is, you know, *first* the gentleman, then Whigs &
Tories. But I hope & trust notwithstanding the *groans of Whigs* or
grunts of pigs that we may have the honour of meeting a noble
Enemy with whom to discuss the interests of the Country.' Whigs
were not a subject for jocularity with the Duke of Newcastle. But the

chief burden of these letters was to hurry on the Duke who was making no progress in financial agreements, and to whom the matter of pin-money had been sufficiently embarrassing; to this was now added the question of a jointure and provision for younger children. The tact and consideration with which the Duke of Hamilton handled these subjects reveals him in the kindliest of lights.[n]

> The situation of your affairs, you find, very different from what you had expected; and therefore, instead of from £5000 to £6000 per annum, which you had intended for Lincoln, you find yourself constrained to limit yourself to £3000 per annum – to which I reply – I am convinced of your disposition to do everything that is liberal; and therefore to whatever sum you limit the income of your Son, I am persuaded that you are guided by the necessity of the case. My daughter looks to the Individual & estimates Lincoln solely by his virtuous & valuable qualities. I cannot after your statement, add a syllable, nor am I disposed to do it. In regard to the pin-money for my daughter; you appear disposed to limit it to £500 per annum, instead of (what was talked of) nearly double that sum. To be candid I think she would require from £600 to £700. Ladies however understand these matters better than we do; & there would naturally be an augmentation in the event of her surviving you. But there are two subjects, nearly overlooked by us, of more material importance, & to which I must now call your attention. The one is a jointure, & the other a provision for younger children. A jointure too, whatever it might be, would naturally be increased under the same circumstances as pin-money. If there should be a sort of convention in your family in regard to a provision for widows, that provision would require to be considered likewise. Again the provision for younger children will have to be considered, and this I suppose must be settled by you & Lincoln when ye resettle & reintail the family property upon him & his issue. But more I cannot do, except the offering them a habitation. When can all this be reduced to legal forms? You will, I am sure, be more than liberal, & I shall not, I am sure, question your liberality. I only seek for the comfort & advantage of your family, & to promote that comfort & advantage I wish to limit & define the situation & existence my daughter is to have in it. Only be

kind enough to let me know when you will be ready, & I will not be behindhand.

From Scotland throughout October hints of impatience were felt at Clumber. And having been kept thoroughly acquainted with every misfortune of health affecting each member of the family, the Duke of Hamilton discharged with gallantry a graceful postscript: 'I grieve to learn that your fair daughters have not been well.'

Matters dragged on a few weeks longer; the Duchess by now in London – having 'sent for some Leamington waters' and drinking them with great success – resolved the terms herself, while dropping the unpalatable threat that it was preferable to settle things between themselves 'than to refer it to Counsel'; 'my duke is willing to come forward with a 1000£ provision for the children in the event of Susan's being left a widow during your life time, & I am sure you are as liberally inclined as he is.' The Duke of Newcastle, reserving his right over his own one thousand pounds' provision, brought forth a '"Tit for Tat" as they say, my dear Duke. Your decision about the 1000£ "to cease in case of Susan's marrying again"' was reasonable when balanced against adjustments of her own. All contingencies had now been scrutinized and financial precautions taken. Births, deaths, widowhood, were catered for. Alone divorce had no identity.

3
Marriage and a Love-letter

There was cause for haste; Lincoln's bright future depended not only on domestic felicity but on winning his Parliamentary seat, and between the one rapturous event and the disturbing uncertainty of the other there existed a bare three weeks. The wedding was fixed for November 26th. Mr Brown, with power in his hands to manipulate Hamilton financial strings, journeyed south, and writing from Burlington Hotel, Cork Street, thanked the Duke of Newcastle for the 'very condescending way' in which he had been received at Clumber. The Duchess, now busy with preparations for the wedding ceremony at Hamilton Palace, gave the Duke a hint for a wedding present. 'As you desire me to *suggest* a cadeau for your future Daughter, I venture to propose that it should be an India Shawl. Susan has seen a white one for a Hundred and twenty guineas' which she was anxious to possess and, presented to her by the Duke, it would be a delightful surprise. 'I hope you will not scruple to say *No* if my idea should appear indiscreet'; it was her confidence in his candour which had made her bold. And while seeing everything 'couleur de rose' she could not but confide that 'I cling to Susan's happiness, more even than to herself, and pray you will believe that my too sensitive nature only makes me anxious, but not *exigeante*. If Susan justifies the pride with which I say "There's my child", she will more than repay the sacrifice I am about to make. I shall watch over her with my mind's eye, and bless God that if I should be removed from this world of care, my treasure is safe in port. Believe me always faithfully & affly your obliged SEHB&C.'[n]

With these laudable sentiments ringing in his ears, the Duke of Newcastle made his preparations for reaching Scotland. Although judging the distance to be 'altogether formidable' at that time of year, he expected to accomplish the journey well within three days (Lincoln having gone earlier). Instead of the Settle and Kendal road, his host advised him to 'get immediately into the great north road to Carlisle', and accordingly he reached there in the late evening having been travelling fifteen hours. Breakfasting the next day at Gretna Green, he found to his astonishment the innkeeper to be a man once his valet, who since the blacksmith's death himself married eloping couples – in the Duke's view a 'most infamous business which ought to be stopt by law'. Following upon his arrival at Hamilton Palace came very unsettling news indeed: 'Lord Douglas has taken the small pox at Oxford, altho' he has been vaccinated.' This was disturbing enough, but the Duchess was 'quite upset by the intelligence', plans were overturned, and the ceremony postponed until the 27th: all matters destructive to the Duke's comfort. But his surroundings deeply impressed him. 'This is a noble house. Everything on the grandest scale & in the most perfect taste. It is difficult to know which most to admire, the design or the execution of the work, both are so admirable. I never saw so good, grand & faultless a house. It is truly palatial.'[n] The wedding day brought its quota of emotions. 'The poor Duchess bore up admirably & fortified herself for parting with her only & beloved daughter', and the Duke of Newcastle himself was so much affected that he could not master himself; 'a thousand different thoughts & recollections came into my mind & touched the tenderest cords.' His 'dear & admirable Son' was married to Susan, first according to the forms of the Established Church, and then by a clergyman of the Scotch Church. As they set off for their honeymoon, the Broose, a survival of a primitive marriage custom, was enacted, in which four to five horsemen not escorting the carriage took part at full gallop. A bottle of whisky, a toasting of the bride in the road, and other attentions were part of this ancient practice. The day closed on a warm note of approval in the Duke's diary: 'Dinners were given to all the Duke of Hamilton's tenantry, in the stables & outhouses, the arrangements were excellent & the supply most bountiful. One could *hear* the effects of it untill a late hour. The Gentlemen & superior tenants & vassals had a dinner in the town, in all about 2000 were dined. Nothing was wanting to do honor to the occasion or credit to the exalted owners of this magnificent place.' On the morning of the following day he received a few lines from Lincoln – 'he tells me he is supremely happy.' On December 17th, Lincoln, 'my matchless Son', twenty-one and married, was elected to his seat in Parliament.

Midway through the following year Lincoln confided to his father that 'his dear wife was in the family way & that her confinement may

be expected in January, if', added the Duke (for anticipation of cata-
strophe could never be disregarded), 'all goes well.' Suzie was enjoy-
ing her London season; she had been presented at a Drawingroom
which was also attended by her father-in-law and his two daughters.
An excursion to Stratfield Saye in June could be counted a success,
though the Duke thought the house 'wretched & in a melancholy
looking state. We saw the old horse (Copenhagen) which the Duke of
Wellington rode on the 18th [June] at the battle of Waterloo – he is
now 25 & evidently like his master declining in his powers & losing
flesh.'[n] Less successful was a Court Ball at which Queen Adelaide
danced with the Duke of Orléans, and the Duke of Brunswick. 'We
do not understand', wrote the Duke, 'a dancing Queen. I own that I
think it would be far better otherwise.' As the year closed his affection and esteem for Susan were unbounded. 'She seems to unite
everything in herself. God preserve her and bring her well through
her perils.' Any fears for her confinement, and they were many, were
dispersed at the beginning of 1834 by the happy news of the birth of
a boy, Henry, and of Susan's good health and fine spirits. He was preoccupied by the matter of a title for his little grandson 'who has none
& therefore can bear none & must be plain Mr Clinton which does
not seem to be what it should be. I applied to Lord Liverpool once to
obtain from the King a third title but he refused me & I certainly was
affronted, for the favor is a very small one. It is most disagreeable to
stir in such matters but it looks so oddly to see my grandson called by
no title that I am obliged to try to have the awkwardness obviated.'[n]
His failure to obtain it only aggravated his worries; Suzie was ill a
good deal of the year with pains 'which go through to her back and
bring on fainting fits. It may be incipient pregnancy, but those that
are about her think not.' By August he was ascribing her sickness to
her having imprudently given herself a cold 'at a breakfast at Sion,
sitting out on the wet grass, which probably caused a check to the
usual state of females. There is an affection of the womb which
causes great pain, & latterly after the attacks her head does not
retain its energy & she wanders & is for a time unconscious.'[n]

This latest development may have been caused by an ovarian cyst
which persisted until the following year. But there were more fun-
damental issues at stake than Susan's illness and the vexations of the
want of a third title. At the end of 1833, a year after Lincoln's marriage, two entries in the diary within a week of each other reveal a

disquieting, if unnamed, circumstance. 'This has been a grievous &
afflicting day to me, I will not state wherefore but it strikes at the
root of my happiness.' 'My private grief embitters my days – & it is
the more poignant as it could not be looked for.' The reason for his
unhappiness lay in his son's conduct which appeared to be influenced
in a manner totally alien to his own mode of life and political creed.
Lincoln, though a Tory, was diverging from the rigid discipline of his
father, and under the leadership of Sir Robert Peel was adopting a far
more liberal sweep to his convictions. Peel had accepted the Reform
Bill as irrevocable; he had supported Catholic Emancipation in 1829,
having first opposed it; and in the future was to be the main architect
of the Corn Law repeal. In the light of these betrayals, the Duke, to
whom reform of any kind was abhorrent, regarded him as a rene-
gade. The more Lincoln followed and respected Peel – and he came
to venerate him as a leader and love him as a friend – the deeper the
wound inflicted on his father, and from 1835 until the Duke died in
1851, there were only occasional periods of harmony. Domestically
too, Lincoln had strayed, and this was ascribed to Hamilton influence. Soon after marriage the Portman Square roof had been
exchanged in favour of No. 12, Suzie finding the atmosphere more
congenial and free from the fault-finding which now dominated the
Duke's habitual treatment of his son. After the birth of their first
child he had given them a house in London at the top of Park Lane,*
for which he had had to raise money. 'The most complete, convenient, and prettiest in London' he thought. 'I buy it now fitted up &
furnished, with two months wine, & everything in it for £13,000.
The furniture &c is very handsome & the whole thing much to be
covetted.'[n] Late that summer relations had so far deteriorated that
writing from Hafod, his house in Wales, he roundly condemned the
Lincolns' behaviour, severely reprimanding his twenty-three-year-old
son for having engaged in a pastime of which he disapproved.

Sept 27th 1834[n]

I see that you have both been engaged in attending what *I* call a
Tom foolery meeting where grown up ladies, as well as grown up
gentlemen shoot with bow & arrow & exhibit themselves according to my notion to any thing but advantage. I was very sorry to

* Looking south from Tyburn, No. 25 was the first house after North Row.

observe that Susan decked the winners with the scarf instead of a cap & bells. Such affairs may serve as a clap trap for a certain kind of popularity, but it really annoys & hurts me to see you & Susan give importance to such nonsense, mischievous besides, encouraging a most objectionable display, vanity, freedom & boldness in the women, an absurd folly & contemptible puerility in the men. Such meetings are what is called gay, but in fact are only intended to do away with distinctions of the sexes, & bring them together in licence & freedom to the great injury of morality & good conduct. Once you thought as I do upon these matters, but of late years, my dear Lincoln, you have been much loosened in your notions. I am well aware that it is 'as other people do', & that in going with the stream the navigation is easy & the navigators are well received. But this is not the course that a wise or great man should pursue. His object should be the correction of vice, immorality & all that leads to them. You may possibly exclaim What can my Father mean, what has he heard. It seems to me as far as I *do* know & have heard, that you are by no means sufficiently particular about what you can do, or who you mix with. You are too fond of company and a mixed company. In London you die for the Clubroom or some other points of attraction, whilst to your own prejudice. Think of the community of which you are part, & above all of your wife & family. Your home is neither your home or her's. Susan is very young, gay & free, she is left to herself, you being absent, her amusements & occupations are followed up without you. She is admired, naturally gratified by the admiration, & suffers by the indulgence. Advantage will be taken of a reputation for levity & easy access.

Matters were smoothed over, for in October the Duke visited the Lincolns at Ashton Hall in Lancashire ('neither pretty nor beautified, but very comfortable,' he observed), and found Susan 'quite one of us & is thoroughly amalgamated'. Even his departure was regretted, a sentiment in which the Duke of Hamilton could concur. 'I join with you in your regrets at the Departure of your excellent & respectable father. It must have given you great pleasure to remove a little from his lips the bitter cup that has been placed before them, but his good & virtuous principles are a shield to him in adversity, as they are an ornament to him in this passage through life.'[11]

In early 1835 while Lincoln, in London, was attending to Parliamentary business, Suzie was ill at Clumber where the Hamiltons joined her, 'doing', wrote the Duke of Newcastle, 'what would be better not done, fretting & worrying their dear child by over kindness & anxiety. It plagues poor Lincoln to death & he tells me does a great deal of harm to his dear wife. I know what this is & lament it exceedingly. There is nothing over which I set a stricter guard than this of parental meddling & fidgetting interference.'ⁿ Neither side could recognize his own reflection in the limitations of the other. Nonetheless, the Duke of Newcastle was all anxiety. 'She is still confined to her bed, much weakened & her pains & spasms returned,' he wrote in his diary. 'Lincoln's return from London would be the greatest relief for then, poor soul, she would at least have the benefit of his society & attentions, the absence of which I am certain she inwardly feels.' But quite the contrary: the next day to his surprise he found that 'she would on no account have Lincoln here – she said that his return would "fidget her to death" & that she would like much better to travel without him. This is Hamilton fashion, not Clinton fashion. It is what unfortunately she has been accustomed to see in her parents & most unwisely wishes to adopt in her case. I now find that I have been doing poor dear Lincoln much more injustice than he deserves. I blame him for being drawn or persuaded into a wrong system – but the feeling or origination of it, is not in him. The Duke & Dss of Hamilton dinned it into his & her ears, & thus has arisen this very unseemly & to me very distasteful arrangement.'ⁿ Lincoln arrived, and a bed carriage was made up to convey her to London. The Duke was full of apprehensions, and thought it 'rash & unwise & a desperate step. She is bent upon it – it may succeed but it may do the most irreparable mischief.' With relief he heard that she had stood the journey perfectly, and had arrived without fatigue and inconvenience. (Suzie had remarkable recuperative powers where her own pleasure was involved.) At the same time he had further woeful tidings to impart to his diary: the Countess of Winchilsea was dead, and her husband, the 10th Earl, would be 'wounded to the quick, anxiety & afflictions will almost kill him'.

In May Lincoln was laid up with measles, and his father allowed himself to complain to his diary that: 'His wife does not seem to understand or to turn her mind much to nursing', and towards the end of June, having spent a pleasant day in London, at home with his children – 'a practice which I anxiously wish that I could hope to see perpetuated by Lincoln' – he went further, adding: 'His wife is giddy & he suffers himself to look complacently upon a vital evil – the seeking happiness elsewhere than at home in the domestic circle. It is a vicious poison which affects & influences every relation of life. The prospect of what I see resulting from it & what will assuredly follow grieves me to the soul & eternally embitters my thoughts.'[11]

As so often in human relations, a point had been reached where the participants resorted to subterfuge rather than face reality. The old tale, of what the Duchess termed 'the Grand Duke and the Heir Apparent', was asserting itself. Thus the Duke of Newcastle, the most truthful of men, deluded himself into thinking that he sought only Lincoln's welfare, when what he craved was the dependence of his son, the deficiency of which brought disappointment and loneliness. Lincoln on his side had outgrown parental control, and seeing his ambitions for a successful career within his grasp, his only path seemed to be to strike out on his own, eluding his father's admonitions and constricting conventions from which, rather than submit, he would escape with his wife to Scotland, or Portman Square. He found it easier to avoid his father than to face arguments and justifications. The Hamiltons' influence can be seen as a corrective to the Duke of Newcastle's brooding severity, but perhaps there was too much readiness in taking sides under the guise of 'candour', too much extravagantly phrased sentiment, to be wholly convincing. Suzie alone was not blinded to reality. After the excitement of marriage had faded, she saw quite clearly and within the shortest time, that she was bored by Lincoln, indifferent to his career, irked by the fetters imposed by marriage, and above all, repelled by physical intercourse with her excessively demanding husband. This should be borne in mind and related to her later determination, seemingly bordering on the insane given the proprieties of the time, to leave her home and children for the space of two years. Though this was never put into words, there emerges such a distaste, even hatred, of her husband as could hardly have been precipitated by his moral priggishness or lack of humour, but might account in great part for her unwillingness to live with him.

A series of letters from father to son, written between June 27th and 29th, culminated very nearly in the breaking of all ties. Lincoln's chief crime had been to plan a few weeks at Baden for Susan to take the waters. 'As I collect from your letter', wrote the Duke, 'that you are about to expatriate yourself for a long time, it is by no means improbable that we may never meet again & I should not wish you to misunderstand me.' Much that had gone before was reiterated; a new grievance was aired, that of having seen his little grandson but once in London, and then only by chance in Kensington Gardens, and once again 'in your house, as he was pulled about by a whole room of women'; but the iniquity of going abroad was the main cause of displeasure.

> Susan wishes to figure away amongst the vile foreigners & you are not disinclined to favor the project. I have no hesitation in deprecating the scheme. With a wife, pretty, giddy, coquettish & greedy of admiration, as Susan is; you separating & separated from her, probably attending to some other lady in obedience to foreign law – beset by every snare, a prey to inexperience, amidst people to whom virtue is hardly known, & vice is everywhere present in its most alluring as well as in its most hideous form. I sicken when I think it is my son who is about to plunge into such an ocean of insecurity, into such an unfathomable abyss of dangers. 'You think you stand', my dear Lincoln, 'take heed lest you fall'. Pray read with attention the collect for this Sunday [Second after Trinity].[n]

Having an excuse to write to the Duke of Hamilton who had asked for his impression of Susan's health – which he hastened to define as none the worse for 'hot rooms & trying fêtes' – he seized the opportunity of saying that 'Susan is too young & much too giddy to be abandoned to the wiles of foreign artifice. Lincoln is a mere child & suffers himself to be led.' To his father's wounding, but curiously perceptive, appraisal of Suzie's character, Lincoln replied: 'As you have commenced an attack upon my *wife,* I shall confine myself to say that there is not one word of truth in it & that my Father is the only man alive who should with impunity have said & insinuated what you have.' His father had also charged him with having no family life, which he equally firmly refuted. His day had assumed a regular pattern in which business at the House did not call him from home until the afternoon; sometimes on the way he stopped for ten minutes at the Carlton 'to revel in the dissipation of the Whig papers which I do not take in at home'. Harassed beyond measure he disclosed that 'When we are at a distance from each other I never open a letter from you without a beating heart – it may contain words of affection, perhaps even of approval, but it may upbraid me as a wretch unworthy to live – & this because I have omitted to write word of the result of an important division. These scenes, over which I have no control, haunt me in every action of my life.'[n]

There was no journey abroad. In the late summer at Hamilton, Susan, who was still suffering from the probable ovarian cyst ('the principal complaint which is in the *womb*' – though after this year there is no further reference to it), was looking uncommonly yellow as by now her liver was 'dreadfully affected'. 'Darling Toosey', wrote her mother, 'was also suffering sadly from cramp in her side, poor love!', and she was rarely free from spasms which, when thus attacked, 'her screams, which are tremendous' had the inconvenience of 'frightening people out of their senses'. They could be heard from one end of the house to the other. But 'poor dear patient Darling – she is indeed severely tried, but no doubt it is for her good', though to see her child 'writhing in agony' was almost more than the Duchess could bear.[8] To Lincoln, who had been obliged to absent himself, Susan wrote of her Edinburgh doctor's diagnosis. 'He says the pain in my back is from an affection of the nerves *of the spine & that* is what must be attended to.' She was not to exert herself, but must be '*amused* & have leeches applied *outwardly* to the *very part* which is *so* painful to the *touch*. He disapproves of strong *medicine, and steel* he says is *dreadful*. He says he would be *miserable* to hear of my being in the family way; he tells me that he *answers* to cure me in a few months & "*then* the sooner you set about having a family the better". He says there is a *slight* enlargement of the womb, a tenderness which must not be neglected, but the *back* is *the* great enemy. Ever ever yr own affect Toosey.'[n] She had adopted a new style of hairdressing which her mother found vastly becoming. 'Her hair is dressed (instead of the odious Pyramid) like an antique statue (a *long* plait instead of a short one). Lincoln says it is all *his* doing. I am not sure that total *plainness* in the sides becomes her as much as the plaits but on the whole she looks delightfully, dear dear dear Suzie!' In pale pink satin, taking her mother's place at table opposite her father, or as Hayter depicted her with her hair dressed 'like an antique statue', to a mother's fond eye and to her adoring husband she appeared ravishing.[9]

By letter the Duke of Hamilton attempted, not without slow success, to mediate between Lincoln and his father. He liked his son-in-law ('He pays my beloved Duke the most unwearied attention & a *shake of the hand* is substituted for the *pendulum* now. I am so very very glad', wrote the Duchess)[10] and in early February, 1836, Lincoln himself asked his father to receive him. 'After two years of most painful bodily suffering which my poor wife has undergone and the corresponding mental anxiety which I have endured on her account I have every reason to hope that God will grant us a new comfort, if not a release from her sufferings, by blessing her with another child.'[11] By degrees partial harmony was restored; the Duke of Newcastle noted that Suzie's 'spasms, or convulsions' had returned, which were 'very inauspicious and much to be lamented'. Edward, the second child, was born in August and, of a family of five, proved to be the only one of whom a father might be proud.

The year had been clouded by ill health; the Duke of Hamilton had had a severe attack of gout in the summer while in Paris, and hobbled about in green slippers with 'a cord round his throat like a huissier de la Chambre, nobody knows why'.[11] He adopted many absurdities of dress: another was the conspicuous placing of small combs in his hair. The Duchess was suffering from the 'tic doulour-eux, added to a derangement of the nerves of the stomach', and Suzie was not much better, though her mother shrewdly observed that though 'ill she *cannot* be very ill when she is able to dine out & sing a whole evening'. On his side, the Duke of Newcastle felt obliged to write to Lord William, his twenty-one-year-old son, at Oxford, to ask about his piles. The breeziness of the reply was hardly likely to reconcile his father. 'You asked whether I meant that I had the *piles*. I believe it was, as far as I know of them, which is not *much*.' But very much worse was to follow before the year closed.

The Duke of Newcastle's children, especially the girls, remain shadowy figures, though the Duke of Hamilton would occasionally try to redeem them from obscurity by sending them messages which it is doubtful were ever communicated to them. 'Pray say everything most kind from me to your fair ladies', he would write, '& contrive to come up to town again at a fashionable moment, that they may give a good example to the dandy ladies here, who I think ten times worse than the dandy gentlemen.' The sisters were intrigued by Susan and fascinated by the Duchess, who brought undreamed of sparkle and dash to the confines of Clumber. They were never allowed to pay a visit to their brother's house in Park Lane, for he and Suzie had quarrelled with the tale-bearing governess who was obliged to accompany them as chaperone. In the presence of their father, Lady Canning observed when she visited Clumber, none of them dared speak. Of the five younger boys, the twins, Lord Charles and Lord Thomas, and Lord William made themselves conspicuous in their own particular manner, and in November of that year Charles, a captain in the Life Guards, did so with a certain éclat. The Duchess of Hamilton had two devoted nieces, daughters of her Orde sister, whom she had brought up after their mother's death in 1818. Susan married a Mr Villiers Dent, and Madge, still a spinster, was much in her aunt's confidence, and was the recipient of many of her letters. Lord Charles proposed to Madge Orde, and wrote, as did the Duchess also, for his father's consent. The Duke's diary entry: 'Charles declared himself for Miss Orde, a little miserable poor creature, with nothing whatever to recommend her. I would not have him link himself to such a person on any account.' His replies to the two letters ensured that the romance was abruptly nipped in the bud. To the Duchess he entered into no particulars, to his son he was more explicit.

Clumber Novr 19th 1836[n]

My dear Charles, Various & numerous as have been the incidents in my life which have caused me astonishment, nothing I must plainly own has given me more inexpressible astonishment than the letter which I received from you last night. I have a most decided objection to such a union for almost innumerable reasons but for none more than the odious and intolerable connection which would thus be doubly rivetted. What you can see in Miss Orde that is attractive in any way, is what I am utterly at a loss to conceive. Here is an unfortunate girl, miserably & most objectionably connected in every way & quarter, with nothing that I can see to recommend her either in appearance or in any thing else, without money. Georgiana well knows that the two sisters never were favourites of mine. I thought them harmless, inoffensive, poor creatures, dangling about after the Duchess of Hamilton & more like waiting maids than anything else. I am of the opinion that the Duchess' education is not that to form a wife that I should wish to see in my family. As a mother of a family Susan possesses nothing that I am accustomed to consider wise, prudent or proper. As a wife she has done great harm to Lincoln & the Hamilton connection has been the upset of my family. It has been productive of the largest source of uneasiness & affliction that my very afflicted life has produced – & now I see no hope or prospect of attenuated misfortune & disaster during the rest of my existence. I have never been able to induce you to associate with those who are in your own station of life. I should consider that such a rippish and wholly objectionable marriage would be a disgrace to my family & you may depend upon it I would never admit her into any house. An idle mind has induced you to amuse yourself with novel reading, the poison of every young mind & this has led you to act as you have.

Carried away by his son's preposterous action, the words flowed fast. A postscript 'I have not time to copy this letter, pray return it to me for that purpose', was obediently attended to by Charles, who was unlikely to have desired its restitution. Madge Orde later took her own revenge.

Having disposed of Lord Charles in the morning the Duke was ready later in the day to welcome the Lincolns who arrived with their little boy and three-month-old baby to stay for some length of time. It was an uneasy household. Suzie had again been ill which she attributed to her husband's sexual exigencies too soon after her confinement; Lincoln, deeply in love, was already pitifully alive to his wife's undisclosed misdemeanours. Both were anxious not to forfeit the Duke's approbation. The girls were at home, no question of their being absent, and the brothers, Lord William from Oxford, Lord Edward on leave from the Royal Navy, and Lord Robert Renebald back from Eton, were to be at home for Christmas. Snow began to fall on Christmas Eve and continued for three days, lying heavily on the branches and settling on the ground at Clumber Park, ten to twelve feet in places. The mail coach could not get through and all communication with the outside world was cut. For two weeks silence like a pall spread over the house and park. On the 28th the post came by horse, but the continued severity of the weather preoccupied the Duke greatly. He feared for the poor, for the cattle; the hares and rabbits were becoming thin and the birds dying. At last came a thaw, but with it the mischief of 'what is called influenza', the diary recorded. 'It is like a cold of the worst description. Abroad it is like a little pestilence, here it is not so bad, altho' very bad.' Georgiana and two younger sisters contracted it, and of course Susan too was 'badly attacked'. From Welbeck Abbey where they were staying, Charles Canning and his wife drove over to stay a night. Since leaving Oxford he too had entered politics and continued to be fairly closely associated with Lincoln in career and friendship. Charlotte Canning delighted in Suzie's company, but was distressed to find her in poor health. Gladstone, who had been at Clumber at about the same time, held a singularly contrasting view. 'It would give me great pleasure to conclude from Lady L's buoyancy of manner when I saw her at Clumber that she was suffering less.'[12] Nevertheless plans which had been formed for the Lincolns' departure to London for January 28th, in time for the opening of Parliament, had to be deferred on account of Susan's health for she was again pregnant ('I cannot but think her in a very precarious state'). The 29th found Lincoln irritable with his father who grumbled that 'Lincoln is anxious to worship his juggernaut the H of C'. The next day Susan was still feeling unwell. The snow fell silently and softly throughout the dark winter day. 'We are all in an uncertain & uncomfortable mood.' Undercurrents, sensed though unspecified, were felt in this strangely uncommunicative family; tensions were rising when, later that day, perhaps owing to the governess's interference, his wife's maid, under pressure, handed to Lincoln a little love-letter from his brother William, intended for Suzie.

4
'I Shall Live for You'

'A heavy and most grievous affliction ...' wrote the Duke. The blow was indeed heavy as it demonstrated all that he most feared in Susan's nature. But to Lincoln the trick of fate was devastating. If not proof against the members of his family, where might not his wife seek out a lover? Besides, the letter, by its implications, revealed that Susan was not only carrying on some kind of love affair, but to gain sympathy was indiscreetly imparting circumstances of the most personal kind to his younger brother.

> My own Angel [the letter ran], yesterday was the happiest day of my life or one of the happiest – those I spent with you in Town are equally so. I am glad you have weaned the Baby – it is a proof of your love, and I hope now your chest will get strong. Dont have the leeches – the medicine you are taking will weaken you much. Let me have one today – tell me all about yourself. I fear you never will be mine. What a cold set we are surrounded by – if I can get off going to the dinner I will, after the promise you made me. You deserve to be happy in this world and you will be happy in the next. Dont let L do it – rather incur his anger. Swear you are ill. He made you ill after your confinement in Town beginning so soon. I have no patience with his selfishness.[n]

Bewildered to know how best to act, Lincoln, with great self-restraint, appealed immediately to the Duke of Hamilton to come as quickly as possible to Clumber. On the same day his father-in-law was writing to the Duke of Newcastle in reply to an earlier letter which had told of Suzie's general waywardness and ill health.

> I have long thought & said [wrote the Duke of Hamilton] that I thought my poor child was badly managed. A thousand thanks for your communication. I am brooding over it with a broken heart. From the Duchess I learned that you had kindly written to her expressing your anxiety about our common child. She felt the

attention with that liveliness of sensibility that she feels everything; & concluded her letter by telling me that she is offering up
her prayers for her child, & child's children. But I must not dwell
upon this strain: my concentrated affection in our poor Toosey,
leads me to see everything thro' a morbid medium, & to increase
& multiply the evils that appear to threaten her destiny. I am confident that Lincoln means what is kind, & that you, my dear
Duke, are affectionately disposed towards our poor invalid; but I
who live & breathe in her & for her, fancy a thousand floating
clouds upon the horizon, & fear & tremble for the blast.[n]

Turning his pen to more agreeable subjects, he enquired about the
improvements at Clumber, and at Hafod, the house in Wales, using a
turn of phrase – 'I am jealous of your new mistress, that little welsh
coquette' – which in the circumstances could scarcely have been
more ill-judged, and to which the Duke would have taken strong
exception. From London the Duchess hurried to Clumber, the first to
arrive, and was joined by her husband, while Susan, her misconduct
exposed, took refuge in spasms, fits of fainting and pain, unable to
rise from her bed. Lincoln left for London without seeing her; and
William, to whom little guilt appears to have attached itself – perhaps because Suzie's inclinations were too well known to lay the
blame elsewhere – was dispatched to their old tutor, Mr Thompson,
at East Sheen, to brood in solitude over the error of his ways, and to
undergo a disciplinary servitude of Bible reading. On February 11th
he wrote a letter of repentance to his father, thanking him for his
kindness and forgiveness, 'unworthy' though he was, piously adding:
'Most heartily & humbly also have I prayed that she also who has
fallen into the same pit may receive the like blessings & assistance of
His spirit.'[n] At the end of the month Mr Thompson reassured the
Duke that 'Lord William continues to occupy himself in profitable
reading. His Bible is frequently applied to, but I have not been sorry
to see him mix other reading with religious and scriptural. He recurs
to both with great zest and freshness and his health is also benefitted
by the relief thereby given to his spirits. I have no reasons for thinking that contrition is less constant or sincere, and I cannot help feeling that he is the corrupted Party.' Mr Thompson was also the bearer
of a communication to Lincoln from his brother, 'full of bitter
sorrow for his share in this unhappy business, but conveying at the

same time the most serious assurances that the object of his intimacy with Lady L was as undefined and unknown to himself as it was free from all absolute criminality'.[n]

By the middle of February Susan was considered capable of making the journey to London; her mother had gone ahead to prepare the house, and she would follow with her father. When well enough she would be taken to Paris to consult Dr Hahnemann,* whose medical knowledge the Duke of Newcastle considered 'a mere juggle'. To his dismay he found that on the morning before setting forth to London, she had made Lord Edward her confidant, for presumably neither he nor his sisters had been party to what had occurred. Lincoln regarded the information as 'most indecent and improper', and an addition to his misery. Alone in his house in Park Lane, sleeping in the conjugal bed in which he had not slept since 'my dear little Edward was born', the sight of the house and everything in it 'makes me feel much more lonely than if I were in a desert – perhaps I may never be otherwise than alone here again – perhaps I may be removed & the solitude may be hers.'[n] Breaking in upon these painful reflections, Charles (who with his twin Thomas was on duty in London with the Life Guards) came to see him. 'He is looking stout & well except that his eyes are large and rolling which I always think a sign of something wrong in him', matters of lasting interest to his father but not sufficient to prove a diverting visit to Lincoln. Fortunately the Duke's despondent interest was aroused in another quarter, for his friend Lord Winchilsea, who had been widowed not long ago, 'is married to Miss Bagot. I doubt the wisdom of the step. Young, handsome, used to a court & 20 years junior to him, his peace may be disturbed, tho' I sincerely hope for the reverse.' Lady Winchilsea would later show her colours.

At Portman Square doctors were agreed as to the 'hysterical nature' of Suzie's complaint (to which Mr Thompson referred as 'imaginary derangements'); leeches were applied internally; the old liver affection, and now fever, were predominant. To Lincoln, every day seemed to inflict new wounds. He had with him his children ('my dear little men are tolerably well, tho' both have still colds'), but rumours were abroad, and he found nothing so painful as the society of those 'acquainted with my sorrows. I mean of course the D. &

---

* The celebrated German founder of homoeopathy. He was now eighty-two.

Dss. Oh that I could sleep over the next six months.' Despite his misery he was not blind to where his duty lay. He would go over to Paris for a week in the Parliamentary Easter recess to lecture Suzie and moralize. 'That will amply suffice for all serious conversation and I should on no account allow myself to wander from *the* subject. Upon my return, I think much good may be done by interchange of letters to pave the way for that reconciliation which I hope may take place in the course of the summer. Of course I shall only go in the capacity of a friend (if I may so express myself) and not of a husband.'[n]

Lincoln, at the time of his divorce, looking back from a distance of thirteen years, could recognize that this year 1837, which embraced their first estrangement and Suzie's terrible illness in Paris, was the watershed between youth (he was still only twenty-five) and happiness on the one side and on the other a marriage in ruins, disputes and misery without end, public offence to propriety, and ever at hand Suzie's all-obsessive ill health. As her absences increased so did his responsibility for the children. The cardinal evil was that he could never trust her again, yet he never ceased to love and forgive. It was probably now that his temper developed into a formidable weapon over which he had little control, and that he adopted a severity in his attitude to his wife that Suzie, accustomed to indulgence, could not endure.

When Lincoln set out for Paris on March 20th to join the Hamiltons and Suzie, the snow lay so deep that it required three hours to accomplish the sixteen-mile journey between Canterbury and Dover; the heavy rolling sea and finally Suzie's distressing condition were such as to render him 'so cold and so dizzy' that his father-in-law undertook to write word to Clumber from the Hotel de Montmart, rue de Bourbon, in his stead, saying that Lincoln would be explaining on the morrow in detail 'what has left us all to day in a sort of stupor. The Duchess & all of us are half dead.' What Lincoln had to impart the following day was such as to warrant gloomy prognosis in the Clumber diary, for the Duke had had occasion recently to chronicle that 'most unfortunately two more Bishops are dead or dying. Butler the celebrated master of theology, lately made Bishop of Lichfield; Bathurst, Bishop of Norwich is on the point of death. No people ever had such patronage as these most unfit & wretched Ministers.' Lord Bath's death ('too much wine has turned to water on the chest') was followed closely by that of Mrs Fitzherbert, so there was small wonder that on receipt of news of Susan – though the doctors promised ultimate restoration – he should note down: 'But this I very much doubt.' Lincoln wrote on March 25th,[n] Good Friday:

> I found that on the day following her arrival in Paris the spasms (owing as is supposed to a chick) had returned even in more violence and frequency than ever, but with this additional & frightful symptom that they seized her in the head and stomach and produced the most dreadful distortions of all the features, drawing her mouth round to her left ear and so twisting the muscles & nerves of the throat as almost to produce strangulation. When I arrived she had been blind in the left eye for two days & only saw darkly out of the right eye occasionally: a spasm which came on when she heard of my arrival took away all remains of vision. Yesterday a spasm ended by making her totally deaf. Another spasm came on which deprived her totally of speech. To describe the horrors of the next four hours would be totally impossible. Hahnemann gave powders which did nothing & it was evident that the spasm, unless for the intervention of Providence, would be fatal. She made signs that she was dying, she kissed me over & over again believing each kiss to be the last, she hugged a little miniature of Henry & made sign to me (she was blind deaf & dumb) about her two dear children. In this dreadful condition and writhing with pain she made a sign that she wanted to write & to my astonishment wrote sufficiently legibly for me to understand, 'I don't deserve it but I shall die happy, God bless you!' alluding as she has since told me to her joy that she was dying in my arms. Seeing the imminent danger I sent out for two Physicians – Wolowski, a Pole (who saved the Marquis de Villeneuve in the cholera), & Koreff, a German, but who were both out.

According to reports published in Paris at the time of the court case later in the autumn, it was Suzie at this point who 'de sa main défaillante de sa main mourante, traça ces caractères à peine lisibles: "Envoyez chercher quelqu'un pour me faire parler quelques mots au sauveur du vieux marquis de Villeneuve."'[13] Hahnemann still persisted with his powders until, when all hope seemed over, Wolowski appeared.

In an instant [Lincoln continued] he said she must be bled instantly or in 10 minutes it would be too late. Hahnemann declared
bleeding was death. The poor Duke ran out of the room in an
agony of despair, the Duchess preserved her presence of mind but
knew not what to do. Thank God I did not hesitate more than ½ a
minute – the responsibility was awful, but I said 'bleed her' – there
was not time for him to send for his lancet, fortunately one was
procured in less than a minute; very little blood would flow out,
God be praised, enough to save her life. In 10 minutes, as I was
leaning over her, I heard her say almost inarticulately 'I am better'
– in 10 minutes more she slightly opened her eyes – it was the first
time she had seen me since I had been here – and she said 'I live!
God has heard your prayers – I shall live for *you*'. Never, never can
I forget those words or the whole scene of that terrible yet blessed
day. I have not attempted to describe my own feelings – *you*, alas
cannot appreciate, for Providence did not allow you to experience,
those which raised my heart in thankfulness to Him & to that Saviour who on that day died for us all. I should add the cause of
danger was congestion of blood in the head: she has now, & has
had ever since, cataplasms of mustard to her feet & ice & vinegar
to her head.

The next day Suzie was given 'spasmodic medicine, bismuth', and
when Lincoln read prayers to her she was 'very much affected. The
Doctors say it is a very complicated case & although the ostensible
symptoms (the spasms) are nervous & hysterical there is much internal mischief.' On April 3rd she took a warm herbal bath and Lincoln
held some conversation with her of a serious nature. His letter continued: 'As the immediate cause of additional mischief is tolerably
plain, so I think there is every reason to hope that with a cessation of
the cause the effect will also subside. I should not feel easy if I were to
leave her until the event to which I have alluded takes place.' 'The
calm of yesterday portended a storm' was the opening of the next
day's letter; instead of the spasms attacking her physical senses they
had deprived her of her mental faculties. 'I await with intense anxiety
the usual *period*. I think that will either entirely relieve my mind from
anxious fears or prepare me for the worst.' The Duke needed no such
preparation; his entries were dependable in their pessimism: 'Indeed
I think her state so dangerous & precarious that I shall not be the

least surprised if the next letter should announce the fatal termination – or a near approach to it.' 'Nothing can be more melancholy,
tragical & extraordinary than the state in which poor Susan is in. I
cannot conceive that it can last long, I am only astonished that it has
lasted so long.'[n] Further harassing news was on its way.

Paris, April 3 1837[n]

My dear Father, A spasm came on with such dreadful violence &
unnatural muscular strength that the Doctor and Nurse and I
were hardly able to hold her; as soon as it subsided she was in a
state of what I can only term insanity tho' the Doctors say it is
somnambulism. It lasted for four hours during which time she
knew nobody and was occasionally violent & at other times
frightened at imaginary persons in her room. This had only
subsided an hour & ½ when another spasm of the same
description came on which lasted 6 hours. One of the Doctors
when this last fit came on desired that the effect of the piano
might be tried. The Duchess played and the influence of the
music was quite miraculous. She was instantly calm & got out of
bed and walked into the drawing room, where after a time she
played & sung everything that she knew by heart – but if she was
not herself playing or hearing someone else play all the violent
symptoms instantly returned. During the time she frequently
walked about the room in the firmest way possible altho' when in
her right mind she is so dreadfully weak that she cannot move
herself in her bed. She is totally unconscious of our presence and
of our speaking & knows nothing but music the effect of which
is, like indeed everything that she does in these fits, quite
praeternatural. I think it is now impossible for the complaint to
assume any new form. She is calm altho' full of pain, but I am
sure from the irritability (so unnatural to her in all her sufferings)
that another spasm will break upon us tonight. I feel myself so
bewildered and have such a racking headache that I hardly know
whether what I have written is intelligible. If you like to mention
all this to Georgiana & Charlotte I have no objection, I can trust
their discretion, dear things. Ever my dear Father Your very affte
Son Lincoln.

It was now the turn of the Duke of Hamilton to write to Clumber,
and in his misery he had recourse to the very human expedient of

laying the blame, by implication, away from his daughter. 'The seat of the physical disease', he wrote, 'is central, & by neglect & mismanagement has communicated itself to the side, to the spine, & finally to the nerves of the brain, Heaven grant that matters may take a favourable turn. I cannot say that I am much relieved from the forebodings I forced upon you more than once. I have long considered poor Susan in a very precarious state. Lincoln's good heart & kind feelings have not manifested themselves in vain. They have done much good, & confirmed feelings of sensibility never to be forgotten, when the portals of another world appeared to be opening upon us. Do not suppose that you are priviligié in Notts, it is now snowing most gloriously here – Adieu – .'[n]

By April 7th Lincoln was still writing home of 'heartrending scenes' lasting four hours, when she then 'falls into a sudden trance. I will only say that I believe it is somnambulism & not insanity, if one can be *wholly* separated from the other.' Three days later: 'At last the event to which I have so long been looking forward has occurred, & if all should go naturally & well for two or three days' he could hope for some amendment. But the improvement was small as the 'event to which I alluded did not go on so prosperously as could have been wished'. He was home at the end of the month and gave an account to his father who again resorted to his diary. 'She is in a state little short of enchantment but so super-natural that I cannot credit the representation & must believe that there has been some mistake.' To his dismay Lincoln, who at present was forbidden by the doctors to see her, was preparing to rejoin his wife in July at the end of a few weeks' travel in Belgium in the company of Mr and Mrs Thompson (Lord William's mind by then having recovered 'its former tone & elasticity'). 'I never feel without anxiety when anyone about whom I am anxiously interested goes abroad,' runs the entry. 'From knowing foreigners well I have a great dread of their deadly contact & contamination.' Pausing at Ypres, Menin, and Ghent, Lincoln was in a hurry to reach Brussels in the hope of finding letters from Paris. He had had a 'sharp attack of nervous fever' at the end of May and was not in a happy state of mind. 'Ever since my marriage', he noted in a journal he started at this time, 'I had contemplated paying my first visit to the Continent in company with her without whom I could never feel any enjoyment to be complete.' At Namur he saw 'a little plain cap which I thought would become my dear Suzie & I bought it determining to give it a berth in my hat-box with the hope of one day placing it on her head'. Arriving at Luxembourg they called at 'the confectioners & asked for ices, & were not a litle surprised to find that not only they had none, but they had never heard of that luxury'. On reaching Paris in early July Lincoln was still forbidden to see his wife, but on the day after his arrival he wrote to his father:[n]

> I received a letter from S last night saying that in spite of all the advice & injunctions of her Drs she must see me and begged me to come to her. I went instantly, and altho' a most distressing scene took place followed by a spasm, the result of it all is in the highest degree satisfactory. Pray, my dear Father, do not judge harshly of my poor suffering wife for her conduct of late. She has been under the trammels & the influence of her Drs & their vile magnetism, and really she deserves the greatest credit for the step she boldly took last night – and I am sure she will find her reward. I have been with her all this morning – alas, as to her appearance, she is indeed a wreck, shattered in body & in mind and looking quite unearthly – but her Father, Mother, & Brother all say that she is as different today as light from dark – and I have a firm conviction that the spell has been broken, and little more is wanted to dispel the powers of magnetism of which I have now a horror which I cannot describe. The Drs are evidently enraged beyond measure and would murder me if they dared – with God's blessing their occupation is gone. Having seen the effect of this first return to domestic happiness I cannot hesitate as to my next step, & as she has prophesied her last spasm for the 21st, I am most anxious that her mind should have nothing to wish for & consequently nothing for the Drs to work upon after that day. I have therefore written by this post for the Children. You will think me precipitate, but depend upon it I am right.

In her present state Suzie was capable of prophesying the date, the hours, of her next violent spasm, and this foreknowledge, being induced by hypnotism, enabled the doctors to have control over her. (It was reported that when, to test her, Wolowski enquired what treatment he should give her the following day, the invalid replied that were she alive she would tell him on the morrow; words which 'glacèrent d'effroi tous les assistants'.)[14] After these circumstances it was only to be expected that the Duke, who viewed the doctors as no better than charlatans, should violently oppose the removal of his grandsons.

> Paris July 15 1837[n]
>
> My dear Father, If anything could induce me to write in an angry tone in reply to your letter this morning received, such a tone might well be excused by all that has been the result from the course which you have taken. I did not send for the Children without a firm conviction (I will not say of the propriety but) of the necessity of so doing, and the alteration both in mind & body of my beloved Wife since I told her my intention has hour by hour confirmed me in my first impression of the case, and I am morally convinced that if I had left Paris on Monday last [the day of his arrival] I should never have seen her again, unless in a madhouse or stretched upon her bier.

The Duke having instructed the servants not to take the children to France, Suzie underwent violent convulsions, and had fourteen leeches applied to her side. 'But whatever I may suffer in consequence', continued Lincoln, 'I am too thoroughly convinced of your good intentions not to be sure that ere now you will have regretted what you have done. Alas! Man is born to misery, & God knows I have had my share, every temporary alleviation seems only to bring a fresh & stronger blow.' The children left by steampacket for Boulogne on July 19th, the Duke knowing 'very well how it will all end – it will end miserably'.

Improvement in health was maintained, and though now in addition to other ailments Suzie had a species of tic, it was thought that some gentle travelling would be therapeutic and the Duchess, Suzie, and Lincoln set off for Switzerland. But with better health her dislike of her husband became more acute, and whereas in the case of Fanny Grenfell, when about to marry Charles Kingsley, the doctor declared that 'only married love' would cure her of spasms,[15] with Suzie it was the reverse; at the sight of her husband they became accentuated. On October 4th the Duke of Newcastle had heard from his son at Lausanne: 'Susan better, he himself low,' runs the entry. On the same date Suzie was writing to her father[h] of a row that had occurred with Lincoln, at the same time vindicating her own behaviour. 'Ces scènes me bouleversent et me tuent,' she lamented. Back in Paris by November it was the same story; Lincoln was lecturing and moralizing and trying in some way to control his wife's hysteria, while Suzie rebelling at any hint of disapproval knew she would find a ready sympathizer in her doting father. 'Elle te demande sans cesse dans son délire,' wrote the Duchess to her husband, for Toosey was now also undergoing 'des angoisses morales'. 'Elle prononce ton nom avec un accent déchirant, et quoi qu'elle cherche à étouffer le cri "Venez Venez", c'est celui qui lui échappe au milieu de ses peines atroces.'[h]

As if there were not trouble enough, shortly before their departure for England Lincoln was arrested at his hotel in the Place Vendôme on a charge of endeavouring to escape clandestinely from a payment of a debt of £18,000 allegedly due to Wolowski and Koreff for their services earlier in the year. This was a case of blackmail, the doctors having kept notes covering six hundred pages ('the most horrid statements') of every word uttered, and movement made, by Suzie throughout their attendance, and these they threatened to publish. The case was heard in December, and at the first hearing Lincoln and Lord Douglas were observed in the crowded court. The Hamiltons and he had retained the services of the redoubtable barrister Berryer,* who easily won them their case. They (not desiring pecuniary compensation) paid in fees the sum of money (£10,000) they had deposited in the bank in the early spring while the doctors, thoroughly dishonoured, were obliged to hand over their medical notes, and pay damages.[16] The Duke of Newcastle sympathized wholeheartedly with his son: 'I pity him from my heart; what trouble and disaster have been brought upon him & us by his unfortunate connection with the Hamilton family.'[n]

Suzie was home in England. Almost a year had elapsed since her misbehaviour with William, but her long illness had fundamentally impaired her marriage. The Duchess hastened to Bath to acquaint her father, William Beckford ('M le duc de Beyford' as the French newspapers obligingly called him),[17] of his granddaughter's health, and while there received from Suzie one of her self-pitying letters which she forwarded to her husband, adding a few lines of her own.[h] 'Lis la déchirante lettre de note bien aimée, et tes larmes couleront là où les miennes sont tombées.'

---

* Earlier that year Greville, in his *Memoirs*, referred to Berryer as 'dark, stout, countenance very intelligent, with a cheerful, cunning, and rather leering look, such as a clever Irish priest might have'. (iii, 339).

You must know [wrote Suzie] that when once the flame of love is *extinguished* it is rarely to be kindled once more. I *did* love tenderly, & would have done all, & *did* do every thing in my power to please, in return I met with indifference, ill temper, & unkindness, & tho' *God knows* I *respect*, I *cannot* love. There are words, looks & impressions which *none* but me can have seen, which I never would, & which I never shall name.

However, appearances were maintained, if only in correspondence, for when Suzie was at Leamington for her health in March 1838 (where, according to her father-in-law she had '4 dozen leeches applied in the first instance, then 1 dozen, & afterwards 4 dozen more, & lastly a blister') her mother, in London, had seen Lincoln ('wonderfully harassed and distracted', the Duke's diary reported) and found him full of praise of Suzie. 'She is the best & kindest of wives [he had told the Duchess] & her conduct towards our dear Children is admirable. You may imagine what a comfort her warm affectionate letters daily are to me.' In retelling this to her husband the Duchess added: 'Poor dear Lincoln! He is the most remarkable example of *exclusive* love; in Toosey's place I would adore him. But her "warm and affectionate letters" are *inconceivable* when contrasted with those she writes to us on the subject of her husband.'

Lincoln was in despair, for his father was again spending recklessly with resulting impoverishment to the estate, but with more trouble afoot in the summer he disclosed the 'melancholy state of his distress' and spoke of a possible separation from his wife. The Duke was 'grieved to the soul' to see his son's unhappiness thus 'disturbed & possibly destroyed', and urged patience and forbearance. 'We must try all before abandoning hope. It afflicts me to the soul to see the position of my dear & suffering Son', yet the son's affection for Susan was undimmed, and he appears to have had still some influence with her. Thus matters stood at the end of July, the Duchess ill with anxiety, being entreated to try the waters at Cheltenham or Leamington, though she doubted whether 'any waters but those of Lethe' could do her good. And then unforseeably, on August 9th, after a 'hearty breakfast' the Lincolns set out on an eight-month journey, through Germany and the Bavarian Alps, reaching Venice in October with the pleasure of finding the Cannings there. Rome in November (where Gladstone dined with them) was followed by

Naples, and there on Christmas Day, Suzie had 'cramp in my stomach most dreadfully. Paestum expedition above my strength & the *jolting* road brought on such horrid pain in my poor back & also in my side.' On New Year's Day the Cannings arrived, and Suzie was happy to hear 'Charlotte Canning's voice in the room next door'; they were both looking uncommonly well, and accompanied Lincoln up Vesuvius.

In April, a month after their return to England, Suzie was brought to bed of a girl. 'L is very much pleased with its being a female child. Susan had a very good time. Not so pretty as the boys,' wrote the Duke. Arthur, the next child, was born in the summer of 1840.

At Hafod the Duke of Newcastle noted in August: 'The weather is most unpropitious to health', and felt uneasy for Lincoln who was suffering from 'something of a bilious complaint' in London. He was altering the church at Hafod and wishing for a better clergyman, 'but few of the Welsh parsons are otherwise than low & disreputable & in their religious doctrines, little better than ranting methodists or hedge preachers.' Two deaths occurred, in September that of Princess Augusta ('an excellent person of the good old stock', daughter of George III), and Lord Holland of 'gout of the stomach' the next month. 'He is no loss in any sense, he has long been a bad liver, thoroughly unprincipled', and like his wife, 'a professed atheist'.

A year later (1841) he was still aggrieved by the conduct of the clergy. 'A fierce controversy is on the point of arising between the weak & silly followers of Dr Pusey calling themselves "Anglicans", & the regular churchmen of Oxford. The Puseyites, strange to tell, have made many proselytes & rapid strides – one has just been converted to Popery & it is confidently expected that at least 10 other Oxford clergymen, Anglicans, are ready to embrace it; such an event is truly incredible in this age – but it is an age of wonder.' It had also been a year of tribulation for the Duke: the family ill ('Susan very indifferently', though sufficiently well in September to dine with the Gladstones in company with the Cannings and De Tableys), at odds with Lincoln (who 'scarcely ever is with us above a few days'), and the difficulty of securing a job for his son William. 'Peel was testy, and refused to concern himself at all for him – neither kindly nor altogether courteously – but such is the man & one cannot make a blackymoor white.' A few weeks later William was appointed attaché to Sir Robert Gordon, Ambassador at Vienna. 'Diplomacy is not a profession that I by any means admire', ran the Duke's entry in November 1841. 'A foreign residence never improves an Englishman, foreign morality & habits are so unsuited & contrary to ours, that it is a fearful thing to launch a person into a vortex of corruption. I have given him & fortified him by all necessary advice & I trust & believe that he will profit by it.' His daughters were at home – in a letter to the Duchess, Charlotte gives a picture of their lives at Clumber: 'As usual we do little else than eat, sleep, walk. We play a little, mostly in the evening & *sometimes* in the day. Somehow we are such *stationary* beings that we seldom move anywhere.'

Susan and the children were at Ranby Hall, East Retford, on the Newcastle estate, but it was not until December 14th that the Duke was made 'very miserable by what I have learnt of Ly L's misconduct. I fully expected it, but nevertheless I was astounded as well as grieved.' The Lincolns had been married nine years, and during the last seven domestic happiness had been rendered almost impossible by Suzie's illnesses and irregularities, now aggravated by a heavy consumption of laudanum. Added to these evils was the emergence of a new lover. His name is not divulged in surviving correspondence and Lincoln seems to have had no proof of infidelity, even if it occurred, but he was so convinced of the corrupt influence of the mother on her children that a formal separation seemed imperative, though her charm was such that again and again she beguiled him into allowing her back. Matters had come to a head at the end of 1841, Lincoln in London demanding the removal of the children from their mother to Clumber, and that Suzie herself should leave Ranby ('Hangby', as the Duchess in a moment of irritation preferred to call it). He also required of the Duke of Hamilton a declaration in the form of a letter that 'no misconduct on *my* part led to this miserable crisis'; in return the Duke 'attempted to insinuate harsh treatment, but without losing my temper at all I pulled him up completely & made him *sing small*'. Fearing that the Hamiltons meant to sue for the children under the Act of 1839 Lincoln had sent general retainers to Sir William Follett* and W. Pemberton, solicitor. 'I have secured the two best men & if the action is not brought they will never know why they were retained', but he was determined that 'nothing can

---

* Solicitor-General in 1841; five years earlier he had appeared for George Norton in the action brought against Lord Melbourne for adultery with his wife, Caroline.

alter my fixed determination of having *all* the Children *solely entirely & exclusively* under my charge. The Law gives me the right & it is one which no human power shall deprive me of.'

While this correspondence was going on, an old friend of the Hamiltons, Dr Gairdner, author of a distinguished work on mineral and thermal springs, was writing to Susan.

Bolton Street, Dec 18 1841[18]

Excuse me if I write plainly. It is in moments like these that real Friendship is known by the Plainness of its Language. Flattery is betrayal. You have not one instant to lose. I think you may still save yourself by a complete compliance with Lord Lincoln's wishes. But let me not deceive you. The name alone of the Individual will not suffice. I hear you say there are no Circumstances, no Confidants. Lady Lincoln, I shall not conceal from you that your Husband's suspicions are now fairly roused and he does not give easy Credence to everything that is said. He will no doubt require that Times, Places and other Circumstances should be divulged. The whole History of the Rise and Progress of this Passion will alone convince him that the bare name of the Individual is all he has to require. I cannot advise you to take the first step unless you are prepared to go the whole Journey. But if I write on this subject I must not in silence see you the Victim of a false and delusive sentiment. To that man, whoever he may be, you owe no debt of Honor. Whatever you may have felt towards him and whatever Feeling may still lurk in your Heart, let me assure you that he has no other Regard for you than such as is coupled with the gratification either of Vanity or worse Passions, which satisfied, he would soon find you an object of Weariness and Offence. A Wife and Mother is a person set aside by all but the most remorseless profligates, as sacred even from the Intrusion of a wrong thought. But this man has taken advantage of your known or professed dislike of your Husband, of which you have made no concealment, he has marked you for his Victim and, practising upon you Flattery or other base means or acting upon your kinder feelings by a mockery of sympathy, he has entrapped you into this distressing scrape. Excuse me if I have written too plainly. Be assured there is no time to be lost. Your selection is between Respectability & Disgrace, Comfort and Misery.

The situation was now such that the Duke of Newcastle rode over to Ranby from Clumber to try what his influence might achieve. On his return, he entered up an account in his diary.

I soon found by her own free confession that her affections were entirely alienated from Lincoln and that she did not anticipate a possibility of its revival. She professed deeply to lament her state of mind that she had done every thing in her power to school herself into a different train, that she had prayed incessantly & fervently to God to turn her heart & mind & renew a right spirit within her, but all in vain. She dared not promise to do well because she knew that she should probably err. She said that she would give up the names of her male correspondent & accomplices and that she was to do her duty after receiving Lincoln's proffered forgiveness (conditional) but that she was sure it could be to no permanent use, that 'Lincoln was not the person to keep her straight'. Those were her words. She feared him, was in horror of him, that their dispositions did not suit, neither did nor could love him. After such & similar avowals I found, & I of course plainly perceived, that an accommodation was utterly hopeless. I have written a very long letter to Lincoln entreating him to act mercifully & kindly, at the same time that he acts firmly and justly. I expected to see Ly L looking ill, worn, harassed to death – but it appeared to me that I had seldom seen her looking better or more beautiful. It pained me to the soul to think that such a creature as was there before me, so beautiful, so fascinating, so intellectual – could deliberately make such confessions as she announced to me. Besides how such a person who is really a good & attentive mother could almost unmoved contemplate an eternal separation from 4 of the most lovely and loveable children I ever beheld – or that such a one who values position should forgo & sacrifice all its advantages & which her present situation gives her, merely to indulge in a sinful propensity.[n]

The Duke conscientiously went again the following day, and 'fulfilled my wretched task'. He tried every argument he could devise to move Susan's heart, 'but utterly in vain. There seems to be something lurking behind & a delusion existing which so entirely preoccupies her mind, as to make her insensible to all but the morbid desire to escape from Lincoln "at all risks" as she expressed herself at leaving home, children, degradation, loss of position, all she has made up her mind to lose for the sole gain of being away from her husband & to possess the liberty of going her own way.' He learned while he was there that 'Ly L takes scarcely any nourishment, & that all in the house have been much concerned. Within these few days two large bottles that they suspect to be laudanum has been sent for & bought from the chemist's. I am convinced that Ly L subsists upon laudanum & other stimulants & sedatives.' To which, on almost the last day of this unhappy year, Lincoln replied: 'The laudanum ought at all hazards to be taken away. As long as she has those bottles she will not be a reasonable creature. Her Maid *(knowing* her tendency) ought never to have given them.'[n]

5
Anglesea Ville

The new year, 1842, opened inauspiciously, though Lincoln, heartened by Sir William Follett's opinion that 'it would be hardly possible (looking to the circumstances)' for any judge to give his wife custody of the children, was proposing to take a small house, 19 Whitehall Place, (that in Park Lane being let) which would 'just hold me and my poor little ones'. He had been recently appointed First Commissioner for Woods and Forests, and 'being almost opposite my Office they will be constantly under my eye and nobody can readily go to the House without my seeing them – the door being in view of my desk.' On January 5th he told his father of a most untimely command to Windsor Castle to make preparations for the christening of the Prince of Wales later in the month. So aware was he of the irony of the purpose of the visit (for anything attendant on the birth of a child was now painful to him) that it is not impossible that Susan's present illness was the result of a miscarriage. (It seems unlikely, given the Duke's willingness to see her, that the child would have been the consequence of an impropriety.)

> My dear Father, Last evening I received orders to go to Windsor today and to remain over tomorrow. You may easily conceive the misery of this – I feel as if I was going to be hanged. Under any circumstances a bore, it is under the present perfect pain – having refused to go even to dine with Gladstone or any intimate friend to be thus publicly impaled is *almost* an aggravation of other miseries. If half the truth could be made known I think I might claim exemption from having to prepare for a *christening*.[n]

Suddenly, in the now almost predictable manner of this strange ménage, Suzie wrote her husband a letter 'so becoming in every respect, so submissive, so fully acquitting Lincoln of misconduct, expressing such proper feelings with respect to her own future conduct', that Sir Robert Peel, to whom Lincoln had shown a copy of the letter advised him to 'overlook and forget all that is passed ... I

saw before I had done speaking that he had come to the same conclusion in his own mind, and that he was greatly relieved by my
advice ... I only fear one thing, namely that after all, Lady Lincoln's
letter may not be sincere ... His father has behaved admirably.' In a
second letter Peel confided to his wife that he feared the Lincolns'
'prospects of happiness are very small ... I am afraid from what I
have subsequently heard that there has been more, at earlier periods
since their marriage, to make him dissatisfied with her conduct. I
have always feared a part of her strangeness arose from the mind.
She is now in a very excited state and has taken great quantities of
laudanum of late.'[19]

Lincoln arrived at Clumber, not a little put out to find that Suzie
wished that a little time should be given to her before 'they meet
again to live together', and that 'agitation might destroy her'. 'A
Hamilton seems differently constituted to other people,' the Duke of
Newcastle muttered into his diary. 'Her parents are her curse.' By
degrees she regained strength though her maid had frequently
'expected to find her dead in bed', and the Duke anticipated 'nothing
good from her', which melancholy prognostic was fully justified by
events.

To the Hamiltons, in the unhappy position of recognizing that
their daughter was unlikely ever to live in harmony with her husband, a separation, provided it were an amicable one, may have
seemed the best course for Suzie to adopt; this would save their face,
and enable her to retain the children. By May the Lincolns were tem-
porarily at 14 Carlton House Terrace (next door to the Gladstones),
the Whitehall Place house being too small to accommodate Suzie
who had been ill for long weeks (*'nervous* suffering, but alas! very
acute,' commented the Duchess). Though under the same roof husband and wife were living apart and never met. Lincoln, learning
that the 'Incarnation of Satan from Hamilton' was about to arrive in
London, told his father that though the Hamiltons might hope for an
amicable separation, 'no power on earth however shall induce me to
accede to this, and my bitter revenge is the earnest hope that all parties may live long enough to repent of a struggle between base trick-
ery & heartlessness on the one side and straightforward conduct and
generosity on the other. Lady Lincoln has not dined downstairs for
four days, but appears at the Children's dinner in the diningroom.
And yet she expects the *respect* of my servants!'[n]

On arrival in Portman Square the Duke of Hamilton wrote to Clumber, requesting to know when the Duke would be in London, as it was essential for the two fathers to discuss 'the painful subject of my poor daughter's alarming situation. I cannot by my silence, sanction the gradual decay of mind & body of her, in whom I live and breathe.' Some arrangement should be made to 'to mitigate the wounded sensibilities of the parties, and save our respective families from publick animadversion'.[n]

The Duke of Newcastle came up to London for the purpose of seeing Susan, and Lincoln, who had by now got the measure of her illnesses, put the Duke on his guard 'against appearances of suffering – every thing will be prepared to excite your sympathy & play upon your feelings. If she knocks under & I forgive, I must & will insist upon her Parents interference utterly & entirely ceasing.' Earlier he had written to his father: 'Her nervous headaches have become apparently a settled habit & the slightest cause – and often apparently no cause at all – bring one of them on.'[n]

The Duke, at Carlton House Terrace, found her 'exceedingly reduced & in a pitiable condition'. As she was 'attacked by spasms & faintings which happen perpetually' he could not enter into serious conversation. The next day he called again, and to 'my utter surprise I found that what had been represented as dangerous illness & confinement to bed for a month had in no degree mollified her feelings. The point which she wished to gain is to go away somewhere & not again to return to live with Lincoln until she feels disposed so to do. She says that her mind is made up upon the point & that nothing else will satisfy her. She says she cannot live with Lincoln. I say that is her own fault & not his. In short I see so dogged a determination to persist in error & evil that there is no hope whatsoever of reform. I now give up the case with deep sorrow that Lincoln should have ever had the misfortune to be united to such a woman.'[n] To this entry he added another a few days later, berating Lincoln for being so entirely engrossed in the 'Office & politics of his party that he hardly allows himself to think upon any other subject'. But life at home was one he could not escape. Whether Suzie was under the spell of a new infatuation or whether it was the last year's gallant, she was once again in a scrape and her husband was aware of it. Under the same roof letters passed between them almost daily, Suzie determined on departure: 'Here have I been for more than a month stretched on the bed of sickness suffering torture in body & mind without the alleviation of one single token of compassion or interest on your part.' She begged for a temporary change of air to regain her health, to which Lincoln, signing himself 'Your injured husband', reminded her that he had before consented to such a plan as a 'measure of mental remedy' which had lamentably failed, and that a 'reformation of heart and mind' was essential.[20] For a month this acrimonious exchange of letters continued, Suzie becoming more desperate, Lincoln more stubborn, the July heat more oppressive. Even the Hamiltons seemed to have abandoned their daughter. 'It is pretty clear', Lincoln wrote to his father, 'that the Parents finding me firm & being thwarted in all their plans, now shrink from the responsibility of removing her & endeavour to persuade her to succumb. This only increases their baseness – they encourage her in her course of wilfulness as long as they think they can turn it to account and then at the last moment desert her.'[n] Susan now tried her trump card. 'Once more I venture to implore you to pause ere you reject my earnest entreaty to be allowed time to recruit my health. Ask my Doctors they will tell you that I *ought to avoid all excitement*. Let me then go to the sea with my children. I only ask for this change *now* to enable me *afterwards* to resume my duties at home. I do not ask for amusement I wish for nothing but peace & quiet to restore my shattered health. You can scarcely imagine *how* ill I am, for God's sake have compassion on me.'[21] To this she received no answer and was obliged to send a letter downstairs a few days later acquainting her husband that she was taking upon herself the responsibility of leaving his roof and going to Anglesea Ville, but as soon as she was sufficiently recovered 'I will return to you & to my beloved Children, anxious to resume my Domestic duties.' His reply left her in no doubt as to the future. 'I know from your Doctors that what you propose to do is *not necessary* for your health. I have forbidden it. You must then abide the certain consequences of your wicked obstinacy and disobedience. You talk of returning! Understand me – if once you go, you *never shall* return, or ever see the Children you now wilfully desert in order to indulge your own perverse will and evil passions. You know *all* the consequences of your act – you have heard them all. You have found me for *eight* long years *merciful &* generous – you will now find me *firm* and *inexorable*. Lincoln.'[22]

Anglesea Ville in this summer of 1842 was a small and fairly modern watering-place near Gosport, its first stone having been laid in 1826. A handsome terrace overlooking the Solent afforded a magnificent view towards Cowes and Ryde. Here, Madge Orde, Suzie's first cousin, who some years earlier had caught the fancy of Lord Charles – to his father's disgust – had procured a house for Susan. She was in London, staying next door to the Lincolns, and had smuggled laudanum into her cousin's bedroom, when Lincoln charged her with duplicity on both counts. 'Lincoln you have wronged me!' ran her reply the same day (August 12th). 'Solemnly do I assure you I never brought laudanum to Susan.' It had been ordered from Dinneford's, New Bond Street, for herself as a remedy for violent pain in head and face. The house had been taken to promote Suzie's 'being respectably accommodated', since her mind was unalterably determined on such a course. 'I again say it & say it with *sorrow* only – *you have wronged me!*'[23] The atmosphere was explosive: Lincoln, sullen now, and obdurate, was at pains to protect his children, though the two eldest would have sensed something amiss; Suzie, her nerves at breaking point, had only the hysterical Madge as her confidante. In the country the Duke of Newcastle was gloomily assessing his vast expenditure and noting that Gladstone's sister 'had renounced her Protestant faith & has become a convert to Popery. She is now serving her novitiate in a *Nunnery*. It is very deplorable that such things should happen in England.'[n]

On the morning of August 19th, the day of her escape, Suzie wrote three letters: to her husband ('Lincoln! you have obliged me to act for myself'), to her father-in-law, and a melodramatic one to her mother.

My beloved Mamina. I need not tell *you* I feel in a most *dreadful* state of anxiety today, *the crisis is at hand* in a few short hours I shall D.V. be on my road! The *excitement* keeps me up wonderfully tho' I am *worn* out in body & mind & dread the after effects of so *much* sorrow & fatigue! the wear & tear I have had to endure has been too much for me & I own I feel *not* sanguine as to my ultimate recovery. I am a wreck indeed & broken hearted, but Mamina dearest dear one, believe me when I tell you I never felt my courage greater than now. I cannot add more. I am suffering very much from my *side* but I must expect it till I am *settled. I tremble* at the idea of being *stopped*. I shall be in a fever until I am off. God bless you dearest kindest & best, oh never never did I love you so deeply tenderly as at this cruel moment. Ever Ever your *own own own* Suzie.[h]

A further letter,[24] from Lincoln to his father in-law, was written that day from Carlton House Terrace:

My Lord Duke, Lady Lincoln having this day, in defiance of my positive injunctions to the contrary, left my house in a hired carriage, and gone down to a Watering Place, I think it my duty to call the attention of her Parents to the situation in which she has placed herself. I do not allude to her final & irrevocable renunciation of Husband and Children. I allude to the almost inevitable consequences which must ensue from the particular place of residence which she has selected. Your Grace is aware as well as I of the name of the wretch for whom your Daughter now almost openly avows her illicit affection. I have but to point once more from Anglesea Ville to Cowes to complete the frightful picture. I have the honor to be, My Lord Duke, Your Grace's Most obedt Servt Lincoln.

In reply the Duke pointedly drew attention to his daughter having departed in a *'spring-carriage'* (therefore a private one) and rejoiced to say that she had never mentioned to him the name of a lover 'nor would my ears have listened to such a disgraceful avowal'; neither did he understand the allusion to Cowes. That there was an admirer involved is certain, and that he was expected at Cowes, within easy distance of Suzie, is implicit in Lincoln's letter, though a friend of his wrote cryptically a week later with reference to *'the Captain'* never having left town, and having been seen there by many persons. Gossip originating with the Duke of Sussex credited her with having run off with an officer of the Guards. Though his sympathy was with Lincoln, Dr Gairdner, ever ready to moralize and having known Suzie since infancy, was alone in finding allowances for her conduct.

There rise recollections of former days and visions of a lovely being pure because ignorant, innocent because untried [he wrote to Lincoln]. Oh that she had remained ignorant and had never felt the corrupting Influence of Flattery &c &c for I still cling to the belief that she is pure in deed, in which case I shall continue to think her pure in intention & thought, for I cannot doubt there has been opportunity for the deed, had there been the Intention. Adulation and Conceit will land a woman so near her ruin that none but herself and the author of her being can make the fine distinction.[25]

Within a few days Madge Orde was settled in Anglesea Ville in her father's house and was sending frequent bulletins to the Duke at Hamilton Palace, for the Duchess was in Wiesbaden, ostensibly taking the waters, though her real motive was to further a betrothal between her son, Lord Douglas, and Princess Marie of Baden, whose mother, the widowed Grand-Duchess Stephanie, niece of the Empress Josephine and adopted by Napoleon 1st, was living at Mannheim. This was a parentage wholly in line with the Duke of Hamilton's Bonapartist sympathies. Douglas had been very nearly beaten to the post by 'les soins assidus' of Lord Shelburne, son of the Marquess of Lansdowne – not that Douglas was in any way taken with the lady and had made it known that the only girl to have conquered his distaste for marriage was Louisa Stuart (who had but recently preferred marriage to the Marquess of Waterford) – yet his parents were unanimous in promoting this desirable alliance. He was duly accepted and the matter of Hamilton presents to the bride was uppermost in the letters from the Duchess to her husband, written from the Ducal palace at Mannheim where she was now staying with the fiancée and her mother.

19 novembre 1842[h]

C'est le *Duché de Bade* qui donne le Trousseau de la Psse. La Grande Duchesse donne a Marie des dentelles superbes. En tout le Trousseau coutera 2000£. La Psse a des Diamants que sa GMère lui a *laissée* et *problablement* (comme la Gde Duchesse veut que sa fille paraisse avec éclat à la cour de St Jacques) elle aura quelques belles parures de sa Mère. Il est *inutile* donc d'acheter des Diamants. Quelques jolis Bracelets, Epingles, Bagues, enfin bijoux de 20-40-60 ou 100£, voila ce que nous aurons a mettre dans la corbeille qu'il faudra que l'Epoux donne a son Epouse. En outre Douglas est sensé devoir offrir un ou deux beaux Cachemires. On en fait de magnifiques en Ecosse qui seront extrêmement admirés ici. Nos *plaids* Ecossais feront fortune; enfin sans depenser de sommes énormes une fois qu'il est constaté que nous n'achetons *point de Diamants* nous pourrons faire de très jolis cadeaux a notre charmante Belle-fille. Douglas donnera le nécessaire de voyage.

She hoped that the Duke would not fail to come to Mannheim for the wedding in the new year, for the 'augustes personnages' who had announced their intention of attending 'pour faire honneur au choix de Marie, seront *cruellement blessés*' if they did not find the Head of the House of Hamilton. She named those who would be present: 'Les Grands Ducs de Bade et de Hesse Darmstadt' with all their families, the Prince and Princess of Orange, 'et les cousins de Prusse et de Bavoire, outre de Duc et la Dsse de Saxe-Weimar; la Psse Clotilde de Hohenlohe'. The young couple now appeared to be suitably in love ('il est amoureux fou d'elle') but the Duchess cautioned her husband not to expect a beauty. 'Votre auguste Belle-fille est à peine jolie.' Interspersed throughout these letters were her comments and judgements on her daughter and Lincoln. 'Toosey, my poor unhappy Toosey fills my mind day and night, her cries re-echo in my ears.' She was justly anxious, for would Suzie, free from discipline at Anglesea Ville, be circumspect in her behaviour, and would she refuse all distractions? 'Non – elle fera des folies', and there would be gossip. As for Lincoln ('c'est un pauvre Sire') she feared his craftiness, for he had already intercepted and opened letters addressed to Suzie. ('Quel pitoyable être'.)

During the autumn and winter months Suzie was constant with her pen, and not only to her father, though he had the double duty of preparing the drafts of her letters to Lincoln who received the usual intelligence of her fading health, of her desire to return as soon as strength permitted, of additional demands for money with which to pay her household bills and rent. This involved a good deal of correspondence with her father, Scotland sending drafts for letters to her husband, while Anglesea Ville reworded them in a less conciliatory tone. Lincoln still adhered to his argument that illness was no excuse for leaving him. 'Four of the most eminent Doctors in London declined in succession to declare such a step warranted. Your father and mother were witnesses against such assertion, for I presume they would not have gone, one to Scotland, & the other to Germany, if your life had been in the slightest danger.' His temper was out of control, he referred to her father as 'that evil Counsellor who had dictated your present letter & who has so often heretofore misled you', and charged her and her family with repeating 'base insinuations against my character as a Husband'.[26] This may well have been the case, for in the middle of December Madge was able to send the Duke a 'most satisfactory & pleasing intelligence'. 'I know not if you are aware', she wrote, 'that the Rector of this Parish is the Archdeacon Wilberforce, lately appointed Chaplain to Prince Albert & honoured by the *intimate* consideration of Prince Albert.' The Archdeacon who had been given an outline of Suzie's sad case by Madge's father ('sufficient to excite his deepest interest') had called more than once but Suzie had seen him only on a very recent occasion when he had just returned from staying two nights at Windsor Castle, preaching in the private chapel on December 11th.

> He hastened to inform my Father [continued Madge] of the conversation he had had regarding Toosey at Windsor. He said, without repeating words, he could freely declare it to be a *fact* that Ld Lincoln's visits to the Palace & attempts at obtaining pity & commiseration had *totally failed*. That Her Majesty & the Prince & indeed all, he added, take the *warmest interest* in Ly Lincoln – considering her the *victim* of an uncontrollable temper & a character totally unsuited to hers. In short that she is an *injured* person & fully justified by circumstances in having endeavoured to find restored health, & that none could blame her even if it proved a *final* departure. The Archdeacon repeated these opinions & mentioned Ld Liverpool as having spoken most kindly & most feelingly of Toosey. The Queen, he also observed, is *very* much inclined to judge unfavourably of one not estimated as a kind & affectionate Husband.[h]

It was not without reason that Wilberforce was known as Soapy Sam; the extant journals of Queen Victoria record no such conversation having taken place, though it is quite possible that some verdict of the kind was passed, neither the Queen – nor for that matter the Archdeacon – having knowledge of Suzie's earlier falls from grace. But if Suzie was adroit at justifying herself, Lincoln was no less assiduous in stating his own case, and Madge, though given to extravagances, reported that it appeared he was most anxious to establish insanity in his wife.

Despite his devotion to his daughter, the Duke of Hamilton was embarrassed by her equivocal position, particularly at this moment when any scandal attached to his family might dim the lustre of Douglas's betrothal. He advised Susan to return to her husband, composing a letter for her, which she altered somewhat – for, as she told her father (signing herself 'Tout Tout à vous pour la vie, Toosey'), although she admitted to being in error she would not apologize, for she had committed no sin; should she return she would only attempt, 'selon moi', what duty required. She proposed to Lincoln to 'join yourself & my darling children at such time & place as your convenience & my weak state may suggest. It shall be my fixed determination as I expect it to be yours to avoid entirely entering upon any conditions, faithfully abstaining from all reproaches and insinuations, all references to the past & forgetting & forgiving even as we hope to be forgiven.'[27] Infuriated by her effrontery Lincoln hurried off a draft of his reply to Sir Robert Peel, enclosing Suzie's letter which the Prime Minister found 'most unbecoming in tone and spirit'.

> I have not seen the decisive proofs of Lady Lincoln's actual criminality [Peel wrote] – and therefore I write under the assumption that you unfortunately have the proofs and that they are unequivocal and unquestionable ... But assuming them to exist ... I think it will be right for you to declare your fixed Resolution in most positive terms, right for you to place on record the ground of your Resolution, namely your conviction of Lady Lincoln's criminality and your possession of the proofs of it, but I think there is no advantage to you in the use of phrases of superfluous Harshness. I allude to all such phrases as 'course of falsehood', 'brazen hardihood'. My objection to this is that they weaken the intrinsic form of your statement.[28]

It seems unlikely that Lincoln had proof absolute, for though in his letter to her he referred to 'writing letters which no married woman can pen without sin', and her religious sentiments being 'a convenient cloak for a vicious course of life', it held no outright condemnation of adultery; but that some fairly precise intelligence was in his hands is evident from a letter Suzie wrote to the Duchess. Perhaps the name only escaped him, and were she prepared to make this known to him, he on his side would not denounce the culprit. (Yet it is hard to believe that had Lincoln been certain of misconduct he would not have acted differently.) Suzie had evidently not been prepared to comply. 'Do you think', she had written to her mother, 'that a man *could* honourably be the possessor of *such* a fact (I mean knowing the person who injured him) & not resent it – no – & I am sure my resistance was *honourable*!'[h]

Lincoln's reply to her overtures was conclusive.

> I should have thought that 4 months separation from your Children would have subdued your sinful pride & led you to write (if you wrote at all) in humble contrition for the past, confessing and bewailing your wickedness, & the breach of those holy vows you swore 10 years ago, & the ingratitude with which you have hitherto requited the unmerited mercies you have met with. But alas! your heart is stubborn still & bent on perseverence in evil.[h]

He urged her to take legal action for the recovery of her children. 'Try it then – or if you shrink from thus eliciting the truth the whole world will know that it is because truth is against you, & whilst you can stab in the dark you are afraid of your falsehoods being revealed. Lincoln.' Madge wrote at some length to the Duke describing the delight with which Suzie received this letter (for no one could form any idea 'of the *withering* effect which the *dread* of the acceptance' might occasion), and how her first words were 'Thank God it is a refusal'. Tears of thankfulness fell down her cheeks and she admitted to Madge her '*full* belief that life or reason would have yielded to the *terror* of a return to him'[h]. Yet despite such protestations, it appears from two letters to her father on successive days that she was at first 'stunned by the blow'. Lincoln's refusal to allow her home – and on her own terms – was not what she had expected. Her love affair had petered out – Anglesea Ville offering no compensation in that line – and she wished to leave; furthermore rumour whispered that it was universally believed that her parents disapproved of her conduct and had withdrawn their support. These grievances as well as money troubles were the weight of her next letter to her father. 'I must confess I have been deeply wounded & pained by the misconstructions placed upon your & Mamina's absence – if on your way to Mannheim you come to Anglesea you will give me a *lift* in the world & soothe & comfort my broken heart.'[h] She was ready to do 'blindfolded' whatever he proposed. 'I throw myself upon your affection & protection.' Most of all she wished to go to Mannheim for her brother's wedding. Meanwhile her mother, who could not decide to leave 'notre pauvre malheureuse Toosey en proie aux déchirantes incertitudes', thought it wiser that she should remain where she was despite 'la triste position de ma fille chérie. Dieu soutienne le courage de cette malheureuse et intéressante victime d'une dureté de coeur presque sans exemple.'[h] When Douglas returned to England before Christmas, previous to his marriage, he went to see her, and made it clear it would not be in his interest for her to return with him. 'I had set my heart upon it,' wrote Suzie, 'I had lived on the hope, but as usual it was too bright a dream.' 'Her tears told how great was the sacrifice' (according to Madge), and the Duchess agreed that Toosey's affection for her brother was *sublime*.

After writing to his son William of what had occurred, the Duke of Newcastle, finding the conduct of the Hamiltons 'odious, vile, and abominable beyond all description' had washed his hands of the whole unsavoury business, but not so his daughters. According to the Duchess they had been lending their tongues in justification of their brother, and were saying that Susan was 'living with an officer at Anglesea & L could divorce her if he chose. It is the limit, poor unhappy child!'[h] She considered Suzie's sisters-in-law should keep quiet if they had not the courage to speak the truth. 'Je suis *outrée* contre Caroline Clinton.'[h] Writing to his father from Vienna, Lord William took the line best calculated to please. 'The mention of the new calamity & renewal of unhappiness which has fallen upon my poor brother, forces me to unbosom my grief. I cannot, how can I?, acquit myself of being in some degree the cause of the miserable condition of affairs. Alas! former misconduct is but too well rewarded by present feelings.'[n]

Suzie had left the seaside in the early part of the year, and in an effort to reinstate herself in society attended receptions, concerts and the opera in the company of her mother, and was later sitting for her portrait to James Swinton. At about the same time the Duchess was writing to her husband: 'I wish you could have seen your beauty Toosey, she looked lovely last night' when singing at a party in London. On the evening of June 28th, 1843 Mr Gladstone was at Buckingham Palace for the marriage of Princess Augusta of Cambridge to a German Grand Duke. 'The Lincolns both there – & Apart,' ran his diary.[29] 'Lady Lincoln did go to the first ball', wrote Lincoln to his father, 'but was not asked to the *second*. I was asked to both but only went to the last having been detained in the House of

Commons on the first occasion. I am sure I could not mistake the manner of some of our mutual female friends towards me at Buckingham Palace. Everybody blessed with common sense must interpret rightly her separation from her Children, and her going into Society under such circumstances strikes home to the heart of every Mother.'[n] But Lincoln was telling his father only half the story, for probably to this, or a similar, occasion belongs a little note bearing the signature of 'E Winchilsea', the lovely Emily Bagot, whose marriage to the 10th Earl, as his second wife, the Duke of Newcastle had regarded with so gloomy a foreboding. She had been married six years but had no children. The Bagots were all handsome, Emily in particular being 'perfectly beautiful', while Lincoln, the lonely husband deserted by a beautiful but scandalous wife, with four children on his hands, his appearance no doubt pale and interesting, must have caused a flutter in many hearts.

> I have been wretched since I saw you [ran the note[30]] for your face, sweet as it is, pains me by its expression – Now mark me! I have had trials of the deepest – often have I been deceived by those I loved & trusted, & said in bitterness of soul 'It was not mine enemy for then I could have borne it, but mine own familiar friend'!! Do not then *encourage* my affections & friendship (which now you have for I cannot help it) – if you will in a few months snap the links now forming! – You feel deeply I see – do you feel *constantly*, for my soul is weary of trials! & *Childless* & with *no* object in this world. Do not wake my love to cast it *from* you. Reflect on this note from yr affec E Winchilsea.

But Lincoln had other matters to occupy his mind, for his responsibilities as a father were ever constant. 'Edward looks pale, thin, and poor in blood', and though not positively unwell needed 'general tone and appearance – *bracing* and *coloring*', and he was therefore taking him to Dover, 'being little frequented at this time of year'. He had accompanied Prince Albert to Bristol to the launching of the *Great Britain,* and had thought the 'vessel a great curiosity', but could not believe she would ever cross the Atlantic, being '100 ft longer than our longest Man of War'.[n]

In this year, 1843, the Duke of Newcastle took a predictable interest in the Duke of Sussex's burial at Kensal Green Cemetery ('where it was his royal pleasure to be placed in search of vulgar popularity after death, as during life'). His Royal Highness, the sixth son of George IV, had remained a staunch Whig all his life; he had espoused many popular causes abominated by the Duke of Newcastle. He chose to 'lie by the side of Carlile* the atheist & others of his stamp not uncongenial to him in life, & so in death'. The Duke of Newcastle's other concern was the behaviour of his sons. 'I grieve for their fatuity' he wrote, the chief culprit being the younger twin, Thomas, who with the same unerring lack of judgement as Charles, and unknown to his father, had 'been married by special licence at Marylebone (Christ Church) to a woman called *Brinton* [Gritton] of Kilburn'. She was fairly uneducated, wrote the Duke in his diary, and they had been living together before marriage. 'I shall not discard him, her of course I shall disown and never acknowledge.' When he saw him in London a year later it made 'my whole soul ache & bleed'. Of Lincoln too he saw little, though there was some pretence at correspondence between them, and in early May 1844 he received from his son a note announcing 'old Beckford's death. He had refused to see any of the family except the Dss – but the night before he died the Dss sent to London for Ly L who went down [to Bath]. He died with little pain & perfect calmness – so completely is the latter the portion only of staunch believers and thorough unbelievers. I suspect the old wretch will prove to be far from poor.'[n] The Duchess found 'my beloved Toosey's presence a world of comfort', and ordered three mourning rings 'of my beloved Father's hair in them', of which Susan would receive one.

In September Lincoln had taken his children to Ryde. Arthur was ill, and he himself was suffering from gout. He had just written a sharp letter to his father commenting on his unethical course of business (at the bottom of which the Duke had added: 'Shockingly ill-minded & undutiful to a Parent'), but this had been no preparation for the blow that was to follow. On September 2nd, Suzie, hearing that her child was ill, and prevailed upon by her parents, wrote: 'Lincoln! a report has reached me that my Child is ill! For God's sake summon me to his bedside to watch over him. To your heart do I appeal, let me fly to my beloved Child immediately! Susan.'[31] Disabled by gout in the hands, Lincoln was unable to reply, but sent an answer through Dr Gairdner, that the child had quite recovered.

* Free thinker and reformer. His wife shares his grave at Kensal Green.

Suzie sent her thanks for the relief of such anxiety ('although confined to my bed') and followed it up with a letter the next day expressing her uneasiness over his own ill health. 'I really believe I should have been on my road to the Isle of Wight if illness had not confined me to my room. Lincoln could I be of any use or comfort to you during your sufferings? If so bid me come and I shall be ready.' The result could have been foreseen. As ever susceptible to Suzie's fascination, and despite a lengthy letter containing the familiar remonstrances and stern conditions ('I by no means encouraged her,' he told his father, and only upon terms of 'unreserved compliance' would he have her back), she replied 'by coming here next day – throwing herself upon my forgiveness and indulgence. The change of sentiment is no doubt attributable to the good advice of Douglas and his Wife and the fact that the Duke & Duchess have become very anxious for their own convenience to get rid of her, I *hope* for the best – that is all I dare say.'[31]

The effect of such intelligence upon his father was one of outrage. A letter from Suzie excited similar sensations. 'She says that he is ill and that she has gone to nurse him – a pretty nurse truly, after all that she has done.' To his diary he confided it was no surprise, the Hamiltons wishing to discard their daughter: 'I daresay they do & so would anyone else who knows & feels what she is.' He was more forceful in his opinion in writing to Lincoln:

Haford, Sept 22 1844[32]

The receipt of Ly Lincoln's letter, unprepared as I was for such unexpected intelligence, occasioned quite a revulsion within me. It is unnecessary to comment at large upon what has been done – it is too strange to bear any analysis; but you should bear in mind the reception of a woman who to your relations & friends, & even acquaintances, you have taken very especial pains to proclaim infamous, who has been proscribed your house, & interdicted all intercourse with your children, with no ordinary watchfulness & vigour – who has consequently been excluded from Society, & treated as an outcast. The sudden reception now of such a woman must either stamp your conduct towards her, thus presumed to be an innocent woman, as atrocious, or as the weakest & most inconsistent of human beings. But her character is gone, it has been so publicly canvassed & so unsparingly blamed, that you

must not hope & *you ought not to try* to force her upon Society &
expect that others can blow hot & cold. It is impossible for me to
answer her letter, & I plainly tell you that I cannot receive her as
your wife, & that I shall require my Daughters to hold no more
communication with her than they have had for the last two or
three years. She is now at liberty to do as she pleases, she may run
off with a man tomorrow, & you cannot touch her. You know, for
she has declared it, that she professes to hate you; you know that
you cannot tolerate her many & lamentable frailties – & yet you
suffer her to palm herself upon you when it pleases her & suits her
convenience & artful designs & purposes – merely because she is
awkwardly placed with Ly Douglas, & is become a bore & a
burden to her worthy Father & Mother. This will not do – it will
not answer in any way, depend upon it.

Lincoln's eldest sister, Georgiana, was unable to 'find words to
express' her 'extreme surprise' and dismay, but his other relations
and most friends were more charitable. The Duchess of Northumberland* wrote from Alnwick Castle the following month of the
'joyful thankfulness' of the 'blessed reunion', over which 'The Angels
in Heaven' must rejoice. Susan's return told 'all that one can hope of
Penitence sorrow and affection'.[33]

The years 1845 and 1846, that brought famine to Ireland and in
England the crisis of the repeal of the Corn Laws, gave Lincoln a seat
in the Cabinet, which predictably proved a matter of grave vexation
to his father: 'He annoys me beyond measure.' He deplored his being
'too much like an office clerk and has all the pedantry of a mere office
drudge. It vexes me to the soul.' He was just as disgusted at the Lincolns' being invited to Windsor Castle. 'What an indelicacy of mind
this marks in poor Lincoln; how *can* he suffer such a woman to
appear before the Queen under a mask, knowing as he does what she
is. Truly it is an insult to the Queen, who is deceived about her, &
passes her off as fit for her presence & Society.'[n] In the summer of
1845 the Duchess, a trifle nervously, wrote: 'Toosey is very gay I hear.
I *hope* she will be *prudent* but … Hope can tell a flattering tale.'
There were no outward family disturbances, and at Christmas time
of this same year Suzie gave birth to her fifth child, in Whitehall

---

* Wife of the 3rd Duke, she had formerly been governess to Queen Victoria.

Place; Prince Albert offered to be sponsor to the baby, who bore his name. Suzie's letters to her husband were affectionate and showed every indication of reform. In 1846 Lincoln was appointed Chief Secretary for Ireland, at the same time losing his South Nottinghamshire seat as a result of his support of Corn Law repeal and the strenuous opposition of his father, but with the influence of the Duke of Hamilton was elected to the Falkirk Burghs.

A laconic entry in the Duke's diary tells its own story. 'Sept. 14, 1847. Ly L run away.' By the end of November she was negotiating her return, 'still thoroughly shattered in health', having suffered 'far more than words can describe'. Loving messages to her children abound in the seven letters which presaged her arrival, also professions of mortification at her behaviour, and though 'a poor shattered creature', she trusted to Lincoln's generosity for 'being merciful to a sorrowful sad penitent Wife'.[34]

The time had gone by for excuses, and perhaps Lincoln had ceased to be wounded by her infidelities. Two years later, during divorce proceedings, there was a rumour that her present lover was an officer in the Life Guards, possibly Philip Broke Turnor, but details are elusive. Her return heralded little in the way of reconciliation. By the new year complaints on both sides had again arisen. At Leamington first, for her health, and then at Bath with her mother, Susan's time was passed mostly apart from her husband. 'How many *days* have you spent in your husband's society in the last *ten months,* to say nothing of the whole period of your married life?' he asked of her. Even sickness now failed to rouse him. 'Both you and her mother know too well', he wrote to the Duke of Hamilton, 'how much she dislikes to think herself better & therefore letters which may be written by her direction will possibly not give so good an account as mine.' At the end of May, Lincoln's letter summoning her home – 'You will disobey this order at your peril' – brought her back to London, but only two months were to elapse before the final rupture. Her flagrant indiscretions and the instability inherited from her mother's side, accentuated by an addiction to laudanum over which she seemed to have had no control, could have but one issue.

In spite of a good deal of obstruction from his father, Lord Charles had formed an alliance with a girl from Cheshire and married her that summer of 1848. The youngest of the brothers, Lord Robert Renebald, was frequently in London in these weeks, and the Duchess of Hamilton later denounced the Cherubim (as she nicknamed him) for having, on Lincoln's instructions, run after Suzie, encouraging her to confide in him, only to betray her later to Lincoln. But by now Suzie was desperate for an escape which would finally terminate her marriage, and for a companion in her deliberate progression towards social ruin she selected Lord Walpole (later 4th Earl of Orford) who, though not a singular choice, given the circumstances, was yet an unfortunate one. He was a year older than herself, a man of some learning, who had married seven years previously when severely in debt the witty but charitable[35] granddaughter of Lady Holland, a woman of extreme eccentricity in manner and dress and sufficiently forceful to reject any ascendency over her resulting from his vicious temper and lack of principles. She lived mostly at her villa in Florence, while he, a notorious philanderer, travelled where, and as, he pleased. There had been an outrageous incident in Rome the previous year when Lady Walpole, having unintentionally come upon her husband in the company of a lady in the gardens of the Villa Borghese, was followed home by him, beaten about the head with pistols, kicked, thrown down the stairs, and spat upon.[36] On another occasion he had been known to take a room in an inn in London to watch from the window the hanging of his servant, but his companions and himself*, having drunk to excess, fell asleep and missed the execution. To Suzie, the turbulence of this life, contrasted with the tedium of her husband's uprightness and integrity, was deliriously exciting.

Lincoln had taken a house at Ryde for August, the three younger children arriving there on August 1st. The two elder boys, Henry and Edward, were to join them five days later with their parents. On the afternoon of the 3rd, Suzie, who had laid her plans with 'secrecy and cunning' some time in advance, drove with the two boys to her father's house where she alighted with her two boxes, sending the children to pay a call. Within a short space she left Portman Square in a hack cab, and that evening at Whitehall Place Lincoln received a letter stating that she had left for Germany to consult a doctor. At thirty-four Suzie's life of vagabondage had begun.

* Characterized in *The Ingoldsby Legends* as Lord Tomnoddy, in 'The Execution'. Lady Walpole (by then the Countess of Orford) appears under the guise of Lady Cardiff in Ouida's novel *Friendship* (1878).

6

Lady Lincoln and Lord Walpole

In the middle of the nineteenth century, Bad Ems, in the Grand Duchy of Nassau, held a very particular place in the affections of the English. Later, fashion drew away much of its clientèle to other German spas, but in 1848 this small watering-place on the river Lahn exerted an exceptional charm. The buildings, all with a southern aspect, stood fronting the water but were screened from the heat of the sun by a deep row of shady trees extending along the river bank, at the same time providing shelter to the promenade, the main focus of the town. Here, since leisurely walking in the cool of the evening was the chief exercise, society gathered and gossiped. The precipitous hills which formed the background were too steep for climbing on foot, but a donkey, of which there were a number for hire at half a florin, made the expedition a popular one and a trifle dashing. Small as the town was, there was no lack of entertainment, the newly built Kursaal offering a magnificent ballroom as the chief evening attraction, as well as gambling tables for the more daring.

Lord Walpole arrived there on August 11th* in his travelling carriage. He had left his rooms at 59 Pall Mall and journeyed via Ostend and Coblenz, bringing with him his courier, Noele Paovich, a native of the kingdom of Illyria, who had entered his service as valet a few months earlier. They took up their lodgings at the Hotel de Russie, second only in merit to the very new and imposing Hotel d'Angleterre which boasted a restaurant, the entire establishment being 'conducted on the best principles'.[37] The advantage of the Hotel de Russie, however, was that by leaning out of the south-east windows one could see the entrance to the town and detect the arrival of all newcomers. Perhaps Lord Walpole's windows faced in

---

* Unless otherwise stated the facts contained in these chapters concerning the elopement, and subsequent activities abroad, are taken from the deposition of witnesses for the divorce, and have been made accessible through the kindness of the House of Lords Record Office (Main Papers, H.L.).

another direction or else he was taking the baths for his health on the afternoon of the 19th, but he missed Suzie's arrival. He was fully aware of its approximate date because on that day he handed Noele a scrap of paper on which he had written two words, 'Lady Lincoln', and instructed his servant to ask for her at every hotel. Unable to find her, Noele happened upon a courier, Palini,* standing in a doorway of a house not one hundred yards from the Russie, who on being shown the name exclaimed: 'Why Lady Lincoln is my mistress, she live here.'

Susan had left England ostensibly to consult a specialist at Heidelberg, and it was not long before gossip had caught up with her departure, for by August 9th Charlotte Canning, in waiting on the Queen at Osborne, was writing to her mother, Lady Stuart de Rothesay, of this new and final folly. 'There can be no more reconciliations after this & I fear she will go on to worse. It is quite crazy.'[38] Lincoln had not been blameless in spreading the news. From Ryde he wrote to his old friend and tutor Mr Thompson that 'Lady Lincoln has in the most unaccountable and disgraceful way taken herself off to Germany. Her conduct since my forgiveness last year has not been such as to lead to any hope of amendment and after so flagrant a breach of all her duties of a Wife and the decencies of a Gentlewoman, you will not be surprised to hear that I shall not allow her to return home. I owe it to my children, especially to my little girl, to allow such scenes to recur no longer.' He added, 'I was born with an iron bit (not a silver spoon) in my mouth.'[39]

Suzie had laid her plans with care and to her best possible advantage. Collecting Ellen Job on her way, once little Arthur's nurse, whose character, according to Lincoln when writing to Mrs Gladstone at this time, was 'positively infamous', she also contrived to engage – probably on arrival abroad – the man Palini, who had once been in Lord Douglas's employment. Her appointment with the specialist took place, and the diagnosis was sent to her father. He found 'ma santé bien délabrée', attributing her spasms to too great a 'susceptibilité de l'épine du dos', and exhorted her to go to Ems for the waters. This she had already planned to do, with a stop at Baden on the way, from where she wrote Lincoln a short note in haste to catch the post, coolly informing him that she had arrived 'safe and sound',

* Also referred to as Polini and Pulini.

and sending her 'love and blessing to my precious children'. She was now free to enjoy herself, but much as it delighted Suzie to find her brother and his wife at Baden on a visit to the Grand Duchess, the pleasure was not reciprocal. Lady Douglas was bound by conventions and, particularly within the confines of the Duchy, was not disposed for intimacy with what she must have recognized as a runaway wife, whose conduct was the object of 'universal reprobation' in England. The Grand Duchess however, unaware of the true state of affairs, provided the necessary social credentials by entertaining Suzie at dinner every day and taking her out driving in her carriage. As fast as he could, Douglas bundled his sister off to Ems, simultaneously writing to Lincoln expressing his 'great grief and his utter astonishment at her extraordinary and criminal conduct'.

Arriving at Ems Susan settled herself into rooms in a private house from which she had a 'vue délicieuse', as she told her father, and was paying only thirty-five francs a week against sixty and eighty at hotels, and though Heaven knew it was not going to be very amusing at Ems as there was not one solitary person with whom she was acquainted, yet she was not in pursuit of pleasure. She was seeking only peace and calm, which 'dans ma triste position' she felt she could obtain anywhere but in England; for there she would be torn to bits and dragged through the mud and Lincoln, out of vengeance, would do everything to bring ruin upon her.[h] Towards the end of the letter there emerges a cautious reference to a plan for wintering in Italy, the responsibility for which is placed well and truly on the shoulders of her specialist. A fear that she might not have funds sufficient for so great a journey was allowed to slip in. The letter closed with protestations of her affection: 'Adieu mon adoré Papino, love me always and do not forget me; dearest dear Papino remain kind and forbearing towards your daughter, and remember if she is abandoned by everyone, poor poor Toosey will count on you.'[h] A letter addressed to the Duchess ('mon ange de mère') followed shortly afterwards, justifying herself and referring again to Lord Renebald's (the Cherubim's) attachment and betrayal. The Duchess forwarded it to the Duke of Hamilton, but in the labyrinth of the accusations and vindications he found himself bewildered, besides which his pride can hardly have welcomed the present scandal attached to his family. That Suzie was right to apply herself to her health there was no question, but he deplored her plans for Rome, supposing that she could have found a warm climate without placing herself amongst her compatriots in Italy. 'I do not understand the many betrayals of which Toosey speaks,' he wrote to his wife, and wondered what secrets she could have divulged to the Cherubim that he could have made public. 'Au milieu de ce dédale de confusion confidentielle je me perds.' The Duchess enlightened him: 'Elle lui parlait sans réflexion, pauvre enfant, et il paraît qu'il l'encourageait à cela pour *La trahir* – fi donc! Le chérubin a couru après elle (par ordre de Lincoln). Grosse bête qu'il est.' Nevertheless she added a word of caution. 'You will observe what Susan says with regard to a remittance through Messrs Hoare's to the Bankers at Ems, and until her plans are more settled I think it will be better to delay your kind intention.'[h]

For the husband there was sympathy enough. Gladstone wrote a fortnight after Suzie's departure: 'It has pleased God to endow you with great strength both of mind and body or you could not have gone through what has been laid upon you ... Feel for you I wish that I could with an hundredfold greater depth and truth'[40] – to which Mrs Gladstone added offers of assistance for the children. However, for the time being Lincoln preferred to keep them with him at Ryde, and then to take them to Brighton which agreed with them and where good doctors were available. The Sidney Herberts* had also pressed for them to come to Wilton in October to pass the whole winter there. This seemed a possibility once the elder boys had returned to Eton, but for the moment Lincoln could decide nothing. For himself, if Parliament was not to meet until February, he might go to Greece or to Spain for several months. The desolation of his ruined marriage and the loss of a wife he still loved, and the lonely responsibility of the upbringing of five children – the youngest of whom was only three years old – were burdens of an agonizing kind.

At Ems things were going swimmingly. Walpole having discovered Suzie's address lost no time in leaving his card, and thereafter his visits were very frequent and the constant exchange of notes familiarized Noele with her handwriting. Every second or third day he was sent to choose a bouquet of flowers from a shop, the 'Florist's Garden', close to the hotel, and carry it to Suzie. His first glimpse of them together was going for an airing on donkeys, when he was told to fetch his master's plaid and wrap it round her legs to conceal her

---

* Statesman, later Lord Herbert of Lea; son of the 11th Earl of Pembroke.

ankles from indelicate exposure on a side-saddle. Dinner, which during the first week of his stay, Walpole had taken in his own room at the Russie, was now eaten at the table d'hôte with Suzie, at the Hotel d'Angleterre. She must have found these diversions intoxicating, but people were beginning to talk. Lord Walpole's visits were sometimes prolonged until midnight and although Noele saw nothing beyond their sitting and talking together, he questioned Palini, also Job the maid, who reassured him on the score of their being cousins, and asked him to acquaint others with their relationship. This he did, 'for I did at first believe it, though I didn't afterwards'.

At the end of the month the Duke of Hamilton sent his daughter a letter of credit for £50 which she acknowledged with gratitude and affection, assuring him that his goodness, his tenderness, his concern, and above all at this time his gentleness, went straight to her heart, adding that alas! she could give no favourable account of her health though she trusted soon to be less 'spasmodique'. Her doctor had warned her she must take the greatest precautions, for if she neglected her health this coming winter, it would deteriorate beyond hope or help. In a further letter she again stressed her yearning for Italy, for there as a girl under an azure sky she had first learnt to count on her father's affection, and although the contrast between her life then, so full of hope, and her present purposeless existence was melancholy indeed, nevertheless she would like to return and relive the past, and try to forget the last fourteen years. Since no reconciliation with Lincoln was now possible, she was doing her utmost not to think of what was destroying her health and breaking her heart. 'The deed is done, I have chosen exile, solitude, seclusion, slander, in preference to living with him; this being the case, je me dois de ne pas me laisser abattre – je le répète, j'ai bien choisi pour mon bonheur si j'ai mal fait pour ma position.'[h]

During her six weeks at Ems Suzie had one bout of illness ('an inflammatory attack similar to the one she'd had in the winter at Leamington', Lincoln was informed), which a visitor, Lady Shaw Stewart,* reported by letter to the Duke of Hamilton.[h]

It has been a privilege [she wrote on September 17th] to witness, however deep our regret for Lady Lincoln's sufferings, with what

---

* Widow of Sir Michael Shaw Stewart, Bt, M.P. for Lanarkshire.

gentleness and submission your sweet daughter bears severe bodily anguish & how thoughtful of & considerate she is for all around her. Much as I have admired Lady Lincoln's loveliness & graceful distinguished air from the first time I saw her in Paris, so little as to be carried to bed standing on your Grace's shoulder, my sweetest recollection will ever be for the noble & endearing qualities which have so shone forth during this illness.

This little vignette of Susan as a child in Paris being carried, uncomplaining, to bed, and the account of the woman of thirty-four, courageous in pain and considerate for those about her, might cause one to appreciate her at her best, were it not for a similar letter to Mrs Gladstone which raises a suspicion of doubt. This Gladstone forwarded to Lincoln, who in reply considered that Lady Shaw Stewart, knowing as much as she did from himself, 'should not have gone out of her way to write to *anybody* in terms of superlative praise of her "patience, submission, gentleness, sweetness, cheerfulness" &c. In this as in so many other instances Ly L's natural tact and talent in that particular art has completely succeeded in deluding, and Ly S S has in fact become that to her most dangerous Companion, a pitying flatterer and by implication fosterer of all her self-delusions and vices.'[n] He had little doubt that Rome would be her final objective, and that 'one of her first acts will be to conform to the R.C. Religion'. (This is the first of two intimations of such an eventuality – which never occurred – though perhaps now more seriously considered by Suzie as an ostensible reason for a prolonged stay in Italy.)

By the end of the first week of October Lord Walpole, accompanied by Noele, made his departure from Ems, travelling in his own carriage to the Hotel Nassau in Wiesbaden where Suzie arrived by diligence (a public stage-coach) with her maid and Palini a few hours later. They had communicating rooms, but Suzie's stay was for no longer than twenty-four hours, after which she continued to Baden Baden to some German relation of her brother's. Walpole lingered another four days before moving on by way of Frankfurt to the Hotel des Trois Rois at Basle, overlooking the Rhine; it had recently been rebuilt, and was then considered, as now, the best in the town. From Wiesbaden he had written to Susan, no doubt giving her the address, for there, on the afternoon of October 14th, she arrived by diligence, a room for her having already been bespoken. The hotel proprietor was curious to know who the expected guest might be, for Walpole was at the entrance to greet her as she alighted. Noele, conscientious in carrying out his orders, declared they were cousins. After a stay of two days, during which time Suzie was constantly in Walpole's rooms, they were once again on the road, Susan with her servants in a hired *vetturino* and Walpole in his own carriage. The final destination was to be Rome, but there were several halts before they boarded a steamer at Genoa. From Basle their road lay through Marat, Lausanne, Vevey, Geneva – where after five days at the Ecu de Genève they had to hurry on for fear of being detected by Lord Walpole's many acquaintances, Suzie being the first to leave by diligence. But the lovers, dissatisfied with the mode of travelling they had adopted for the sake of decorum, now hatched a plot whereby they might continue their journey together, at the same time showing a legitimate cause for doing so. On arrival at Aix-les-Bains, Suzie was to feign illness, sending Palini ahead with most of the luggage, while she herself would await the comfort of Walpole's private carriage. Palini was not to be let into the secret, but when a silk dress of Suzie's needed for the evening required to be laid smoothly in Walpole's imperial, so as not to crumple, Job had to call upon the good offices of Noele, who was thus made a party to the scheme. He accordingly felt no surprise on arrival at the Grand Hotel d'Aix to find Suzie there, comfortably provided with two carpet bags, shawls, her writing desk – this had a coronet engraved on a little brass plate and her name 'The Countess of Lincoln' inscribed below it – and a fur footmuff and a fine boa bought at Frankfurt by Walpole, and given to her at Basle. (Having left England in August, and the late October cold becoming now more pronounced, she must have been thankful for these necessities.) The cumbersome luggage had gone on ahead to Turin, but even so it was no easy matter the next morning disposing the two occupants, and all the effects, inside the carriage. Noele and Job sat up on the box behind. The travelling carriage was peculiar in build, for when closed it gave the appearance of a chariot, but if the folding hood was open it resembled a britzka in that there was space for reclining. The imperial was on the hind part of the carriage.

The road to Turin was a long one, with three nights to be spent on the way at Aiguebelle, Lanslebourg, and Susa. During the day Noele would often jump down and walk beside the carriage as it pulled uphill, and in these circumstances he was able to observe 'my Lord, and

Lady Lincoln, playing with hands together', and on more than one occasion he saw 'his Lordship's arm round her Ladyship's waist. She was leaning back in his arm. I was not mistaken. I cannot say exactly I saw them kiss, but I saw his Lordship's face in front of hers.' The stay at Turin at the Hotel de l'Europe lasted five days, after which the journey was resumed to Genoa, Palini going on ahead and Suzie driving with Walpole. At Ponte Decimo, the last stage before entering the city, there was a rearrangement, Susan riding in a hired post carriage and arriving at the Hotel Feder several hours after Walpole. Noele was alive to the reason for this, for on arrival at the Feder (of which Gladstone was later to write approvingly: 'one of the best hotels, it is likewise one with the most moderate & conscientous charges') his master sent him to ask what foreigners were lodging there. The proprietor understood perfectly the object of the enquiry, and reassuringly affirmed that Lady Walpole, though there a week previously, had now left. To Noele it seemed 'as if he [Walpole] was afraid of his Lady, either afraid or ashamed, I cannot say which'. The day after their arrival Walpole was able to move into a room next to Suzie; this served him as bed and sitting-room, a screen being decorously placed in front of the bed. Here they spent the day and had their meals, Walpole sitting, as was his custom when indoors, attired only in a pair of drawers, a loose dressing-gown, socks and slippers. He would throw off his coat and trousers on coming in, and was 'in the habit of undressing in this manner and the Lady Lincoln did not stop away for that'.

During the Lincoln divorce case in 1850, Noele's evidence was of importance, for his report of an indecency which he had witnessed at the hotel in Genoa was the first factual account of adultery having been committed. At eight o'clock one evening, at a date between November 2nd and 10th, Noele was sent to buy a newspaper and on returning, brought it to Walpole's room. He was in the habit of knocking before entering when he knew Suzie to be there, but on this occasion he omitted to do so, and walking into the room discovered the lovers in the act of adultery. When cross-questioned later by counsel: 'In what Position were they?', he gave the simple reply: 'They were in a Position.' He had found them on a sofa beside the fire, Walpole lying upon her and his dressing-gown so spread out over both, that Noele could distinguish only Susan's head resting on the sofa back. So startled was he that without an instant's pause he bolted from the room, closing the door behind him, uncertain whether or not he had been seen. Evidently he had been heard, for a moment later Walpole, in his usual undress and with a very red face, put his head round the door and took the newspaper, at the same time acknowledging it with 'mille grazie', to Noele's astonishment, for he 'never said such a word to me before – I heard him say it to others but not to me'.

In the following year when proof for the divorce was being collected, Gladstone maintained that he was 'persuaded that the last and great fall' had taken place a week or so later. 'My belief is that she finally gave way after leaving Genoa in November 1848, or almost immediately after it. She wrote a letter to my wife from Genoa* [Turin] asserting her purity of intention, & otherwise couched in such terms that I am persuaded adultery had not then been committed.'[41] To Catherine Gladstone, with a character so Christian in goodness, so innocent and trusting, the likelihood of Suzie, whom she loved, being guilty of adultery would have been so abhorrent that the possibility may not have entered her mind; besides which it is clear that in early autumn neither of the Gladstones were aware that she was eloping with a lover. But that a year later, though knowing by then only the outline of the escape to Italy, it seems barely conceivable that Gladstone himself could have been so unworldly as to suppose that Suzie, with her frailty of character, would not have capitulated much earlier – probably at Ems – to her lover's demands.

The letter from Turin, of which Gladstone spoke, most probably tempted his wife to send the following truly astonishing proposal. So amazing was it, that it must have caused great merriment (if not ridicule) when it reached Suzie in Rome.

Fasque, Fettercairn[42]
November 4th 1848

My dearest Suzy, You who know the deep interest I have always taken in you, wont be surprised at all the anxiety I must feel upon your account *now*. When I think of you abroad & alone it makes me shudder. It is not alone your delicate health which points out how necessary it is for you to have some kind friend to *take care of*

---

* A slip for Turin.

you, but you want protection against scandal – dont think that I suppose that this implies suspicion of any kind. I lay it down as a general rule which has no exception. The very consciousness of purity of purpose makes your situation now quite as dangerous, as it does not diminish the extreme unfitness of your being alone. It is with this conviction, my poor Suzy, that I earnestly beg you to allow me to send you a person who may be called a companion but who would act as a friend. Depend upon it, no person can be a judge in her own case – are not we all, more or less, poor creatures wanting assistance?

I await your permission to send you out such a person as I have mentioned with the utmost impatience & anxiety. You may trust me that it shall be someone you will approve of. I know your taste dearest Suzy – only lose no time in answering my request, which request is only made from deep anxiety & affection for your good. You have often trusted me before; you have often told me you loved me. Oh! shew the sincerity of this by a speedy & a satisfactory answer! For your children's sake dont defy the opinion of society. What motive can I have in urging upon you the protection of a decent companion, and here I must tell you that situated as you are, to say nothing of the sad manner in which you left your home, deceiving your husband, your innocent children (alas, friendship compels me to speak openly & honestly), going away in a manner not even decent in appearance, can you be surprised there should be those who feel they cannot write to you.

I have good accounts of your children. Lord Lincoln has been very ill & Nina De Tabley* writes very anxiously about him. His indeed is a life of trial, may his prayers for you be heard.

Before posting this letter Mrs Gladstone wrote of her intention to Lord De Tabley, an old friend of Lincoln, who with his wife was staying with the Douglases on the Isle of Arran. She was in no way deflected by his reply.

Brodick Castle, I of Arran[43]

November 4th 1848

My dear Mrs Gladstone. Most deeply do I feel the force of every

---

* The 2nd Lord (George Warren) De Tabley, father of the poet, had married Catherina Barbara de Salis in 1832.

word you write concerning Ly L, it is too sad to think of one so esteemed, & still so loved as she, placed in the position in which she now is. Would to Heaven I could think the plan for rescuing her, wh your kind heart suggests, in any way practicable. For *if practicable* it certainly might be the means of doing much good. I have shown Douglas your letter & had a long conversation with him thereon – as you may suppose not the first on this sad subject – & I speak his opinion also when I express the reluctant conclusion I have come to that the scheme is inpracticable.

1st. Setting aside the difficulty of finding a person fitted for so very difficult a post, *who is to send her? not Lincoln* certainly. Douglas *will* not, or rather I should say cannot; he is I regret to say, with his sister, as well as with his Father & Mother, in this affair, *powerless*. He spoke, naturally, *most strongly* to his sister on her arrival at Baden – all which was taken with the utmost indifference & no effect produced beyond begging that the subject might never again be mentioned between them, that she had taken the step fully aware of what the consequences might be, & her own responsibility, in every way prepared to abide by them, & quite happy & contented in this determination.

Then come her parents. They are the only persons who have the power to interfere (by power I mean the necessary influence on her), & they, incredible as it may appear, seem quite contented with things as they now stand – nor do I in my heart believe that they ever have, in any way, discouraged, or disapproved of, their unhappy daughter in her blind & infatuated career.

2ndly. I do not think that even supposing the person *found & sent* – that she would be received. These two reasons make me think that your scheme of sending out a companion, impracticable.

Great indeed is the responsibility of those who ought & can help & protect her, & do not, for one must be blind indeed not to see in the path she is now treading all the dangers which you anticipate. I have long expected her to turn Roman Catholic & shall not be surprised any day to hear that such is the case. In the meanwhile Douglas tells me she is in perfect spirits & quite (apparently) contented with what she has done & her present position. Ly Douglas had a letter from her yesterday at Turin on her way to Rome. The servants (Courier as well as maid) she will I believe get rid of. She will probably not get much better in their place – but she cannot well get worse. It is my conviction that any effort which friends may make before *her own heart is touched* & she herself sees the errors of her ways will be useless – perhaps *worse* than useless.

Most sincerely yours

WARREN DE TABLEY

A few weeks later Mrs Gladstone sent a copy of her letter to Lady De Tabley; the answer must have been received with consternation.

[Tabley House, Cheshire] November 29th [1848][44]
My dearest Pussy,* I hasten to return the enclosed lest you should be anxious about it. Alas, I cannot be sanguine as to the effects produced by your kind advice. I think you cannot know Susan as well as I do if you think she could bear to have any one who would control her actions – and if not, of what use would the companion be? I love and admire your kindness in trying to save her from herself as it were – but I fear that your plans will fail and that you will draw on yourself the enmity of the Duchess who evidently approves entirely of what Lady L is doing – as both must have encouraged her going, and *has since* supplied her with all the money she could want.

While I was at Arran she [Suzie] wrote a letter apparently of a few days older date than yours from Turin. There was not a word in it of ill health or concern about the children, *just* a letter as from a happy person who had not a care in the world. I *cannot bear*, even to you my own Pussy, with whom I know it will not go farther, to say an unkind thing of poor Susan L, but you ought to know that she is not supposed to be alone. We had heard from several people that Lord Walpole had met her at Ems and that she had behaved very giddily with him there – *now* they are said to be gone to Italy together. George and I, not liking to lend our ears to scandal, neither believed this nor told Lord Lincoln a word of it while he was here, but that he has since found it out and is sure of the fact appears from his last *most heartbroken* letter to my husband. Lord Walpole is indeed an odious man to be near her. What could you do against so poisonous an influence – I fear very little.

* Mrs Gladstone's nickname since childhood.

Lord W is not a man to stop before he has gained his object – he will probably be tired of her at the end of a few months and then poor creature, her eyes may perhaps be opened. I have no words to say how sorry I am for Lord L. Do you know I really think he is dying. I never saw a man so altered in so short a time. Then I fear for him some plot of the Duchess's to ruin his character. Somehow or another many calumnies have got about concerning him, and I cannot but think that they might be traced back to Lady L's family. These are most delicate matters to speak about and I rely on your *burning* this letter my dearest Pussy. I have written very unguardedly what I think – and nothing but my firm belief that Lord Lincoln's character will be gone, in the eyes of the world, if he ever sees Lady L again, makes me tell you this. I think he claims just now all the support that true friends can give – for *he* is *really* to be pitied – and do what one may, he never can be again the man he was – she has blighted his existence and I fear is totally without feeling for her children. What the Duchess is aiming at is a mystery to me. Does she indeed wish a separation or a divorce – it seems to me she does, but wishes the world may think all the wrong on Lord L's side.

And now goodbye you dear kind thing whom I love from my heart. May I, if I need it, find such a friend as you are to poor Susan. Ever yr affecte CB De T.

What the Hamiltons' game was is not clear. When Mrs Gladstone wrote her letter to Suzie on November 4th, she still required an address to which to send it, and wrote to the Duchess for information. The reply, though friendly, was guarded and non-committal, yet one may detect an underlying gratitude for Mrs Gladstone's faith in her daughter.

Hamilton Palace[45]
November 6th 1848

My dear Mrs Gladstone, I hasten to thank you for your kind letter. Susan's address now is at Rome. at least I mean to direct to her there, as she mentions in a few lines which I received from her yesterday that she had reached Turin, and meant to proceed on her journey to Rome the next day. She had alas been very unwell and was detained at Geneva for two or three days by an attack of Spasms. She expects wonders from the climate of Italy; God grant that she may not be disappointed. It will give her great pleasure to hear from you.

I am truly grateful for your enquiries after me. I am much as usual. The Duke has had a touch of the Gout, but is now, thank God, well. I often think of you sitting at the piano like St Cecilia with your little choir around you.* I am glad my precious grandchildren keep up their correspondence with you.

God bless you my dear Mrs Gladstone, believe me very sincerely yours, SEHB & C

The Duke and Duchess cannot have been in the dark with regard to Suzie's association with Walpole, though as yet her letters to them had neither mentioned nor named a companion. The Duchess, realizing that reconciliation with Lincoln could never now be entertained (though perhaps not yet envisaging the scandal of divorce), put on as good a front as possible.

On November 10th the party of lovers, couriers, carriage, and maid boarded a steamer to Leghorn where two days were spent at the Hotel San Marco. Although, according to *Murray's Handbook*, it was an 'inconvenient distance from the centre of the town', this must have been to their advantage. However, from Leghorn to Civitavecchia – forty miles north of Rome – 'their apparent relations attracted unfavourable notice on board from a clergyman, Mr Ward, & I also believe from the present Lady Gosford'.† When sending information a year later to Lincoln's solicitor, Gladstone added that 'from Mr Ward's report (which had come to me through Mr Charles Harris, brother to Ld Malmesbury) it was a necessary inference that they travelled together'.[46] Disembarking at the Hotel Orlandi, close to the landing stage, they again spent all their time in each other's company, Walpole securing two rooms for himself, although at exorbitant rates.

A rather more judicious course was adopted for the arrival in Rome on November 16th. A hired diligence took Suzie and her servants ahead, and Walpole in his own carriage followed two hours later. He seems to have been surprised at not finding her at the Hotel

---

* Mrs Gladstone was now the mother of five; she would gather her children around her, and together they would sing hymns.
† Her husband, the 3rd Earl, had succeeded only a few months before Gladstone wrote this letter in October 1849.

de l'Europe – this and the Hotel de Londres, both in the Piazza di Spagna, being under the same management (Serni's) and much patronized by the English – and it may have been that recognizing there some acquaintance, she took her apartments at Hotel Maloni in the Piazza del Popolo. Their lodging arrangements were not very successful; Walpole was forever changing his, finally settling in the private part of one of Serni's establishments, while Suzie took rooms in a house in the Vico Barberini. It was probably while in quest of private accommodation that Lady Gosford came upon them[47] 'going about together in search of houses. She then thought the case so bad that all must have been over.'* They could not have been aware of her identity or they might have comported themselves more prudently, for gossip was abroad, and early next year the Duke of Hamilton rebuked his daughter about reports that were being circulated. Suzie hastened to deny them in her own inimitable manner.

> Rome, February 21st [1849][h]
> In my position, my very dear Papa, I cannot be surprised if unfavourable rumours are spread about me. I will do my best not to lay myself open to slander, but there are so few people here this season that they have nothing better to do than to gossip. Nevertheless I lead a very quiet life though I see a good deal of the Mt Edgcumbes. I have not the slightest regret at having left London, and though no one can judge for another, I can assure you that there are no miseries or misfortunes which can make me suffer in the way I suffered with *him*. Compared to that all else is trifling. But let me implore you not to believe *all* reports and inventions about me; no one is making love to me.

There was still no mention of her seducer, and she seems to have pulled the wool over Lady Mount Edgcumbe's eyes fairly effectively, for Lincoln too had heard that 'she lives a good deal with Ld & Ly Mount Edgcumbe'. And though there was an intimation of social activities with 'princesse Rospigliosi, Mme Del Drago, le prince Canino, Mme Potemkin', and 'la maison de Mt Edgcumbe', there was neither now nor in further (surviving) letters to her parents, a mention or regret of any kind for her children.

---

* Adultery committed.

Though she was not yet showing signs of pregnancy, tongues were busy, for Walpole had engaged a town carriage for her with a coachman, and a *laquais de place* called Ercole, and was thus able to take Suzie driving during the day and accompany her when she dropped her engraved visiting card at several houses. It enabled him also to leave her apartments late at night; sometimes as late as midnight. She in turn had dismissed Palini soon after her arrival, probably not through insufficiency of money as she immediately replaced him, but more likely because Palini knew too much, and was talking. Saccomani Santi, the new courier, was such a handsome figure that Gladstone, in his deposition as witness, acknowledged that 'his appearance was so remarkable that there was no mistaking it, his height at least, I should think, six foot four inches and a particularly fine and striking appearance'. There are many references to the amazing looks of Santo Bello, as he came to be known; his beard, his peculiar manner of dress, always a little showy, came in for observation, and in the light of Suzie's subsequent indiscretions the thought arises whether later on his relationship became closer than that of a courier. His English also was extremely good.

It was now March and Noele saw that 'the Lady Lincoln was becoming larger in her figure'. He would have liked to have questioned Job with whom he was on good terms, but since Santi's arrival he found himself excluded from the house in Vico Barberini. So it must have been shortly before this that Job had shown him Suzie's little signet ring engraved with the letters 'S L', which sealed the notes addressed to Walpole. Nine small pearls crowning the top, set as on an earl's or viscount's coronet, formed the clasp of a delicate opening; inside the ring was a little gold patent key. Noele had also seen two miniatures of Susan in Lord Walpole's room. By April pregnancy was very noticeable. 'What alteration did you perceive?' Noele was asked under cross-examination. 'She was rather stouter,' he replied. 'Did that Stoutness go on increasing?' 'As long as they were there; it was increasing when they went off [away].' It was so apparent that she was obliged to keep to the house, giving out that she had had a fall, though Roman gossip ascribed her seclusion to miscarriage.[48] A villa at Frascati in the hills beyond Rome was rented for a month; here they would not be known as it was too early in the year for visitors. Walpole had a room and ate his breakfast at the adjacent inn; his other meals were taken at the villa where he also spent half the night. The birth of their child was not expected till July or August but a suitable place had to be found, and Susan chose to have her confinement under an assumed name. When Lake Como was decided upon, new passports for herself and Job (who was also to change her name) were required. This must have seemed to Suzie the final and greatest lark of all. There had been no illness for months, no spasms. She had left a husband and the chains that bound her to responsibility far behind; her infatuation for Walpole made her recklessly insensible to eventual disillusion, and she was sublimely happy.

But to secure false passports it was essential to apply for them in Naples as the travellers were too well known in Rome, and in mid-May they were on the road again. Noele was dismissed since the one courier, Santi, could be relied on to do the work. It may also have been thought wise to discharge the man who had come out from England with Walpole and who could disclose Suzie's real identity under the impersonation. As early as Ems, Noele had observed that her carpet bags and other luggage were labelled 'Mrs Laurence', and on asking Job the reason had been told that it made it cheaper going through custom houses, for if an English title was observed the charge was increased.

New passports in the name of Mrs Harriet* Laurence and Mrs Williams were issued without difficulties. Later, Lincoln's solicitor questioned whether there were 'no means through our Government of ascertaining how our Minister† at Naples gave the passport in the name of Laurence, when he must have known it was Lincoln? ... I have very little doubt his Lordship [Walpole] applied for the passport at Naples when it was known beyond doubt that she was in the family way.'[49] To this Gladstone replied: 'I presume that practically such things are given upon the application of couriers, or even of *laquais de place* and that the official persons who give them do not necessarily know whose courier, much less whose *laquais de place*, a person presenting himself really is. Further, Englishmen almost uniformly look upon a passport as a farce, and very likely our young attachés who manage this department are not indisposed to act in this sense.'[50] Accommodation was taken for a fortnight at the Hotel

---

* Her second Christian name. The surname was sometimes written 'Laurentz'.
† Hon. William Temple, brother of Viscount Palmerston.

des Etrangers kept by an Englishwoman, Madame Unghara,* but money difficulties arose when Torlonia, son of the great Roman banker who had founded the family's fortune, would not advance the money [300 scudi] Susan had left on deposit. Fortunately for her a Rothschild had been more obliging. Writing to Lady Mount Edgcumbe she told her of their Roman friends who were at Naples – amongst them Lord Walpole, and saying that though she would have preferred to try the waters at Ascoli, her doctor desired her to go north to some baths near Milan. The whole party then embarked on a steamer for Genoa, continuing almost immediately to the Albergo Gran Bretagna in Milan. Here Suzie seems to have pressed into her service the maître d'hotel to act as a kind of forwarding agent and to redirect to Como the letters arriving for her at Poste Restante, Milano, the address to which all communications were directed. (Even when writing to her father from Como, she headed her paper as from Milan.) The next part of the journey 'Mrs Laurence' (as she now called herself) undertook alone, with 'Mrs Williams' and Santi, but without Walpole; he was to follow in a few days' time. The Villa Mancini in the Borgo Vico, some fifteen minutes' walk from the town of Como, on the north side of the lake, had been recently rented on her account, and here she intended to be confined.

* Sometimes Ungara. According to Gladstone she was a 'respectable Person', who had been formerly in Suzie's service 'and had her confidence and Lord Lincoln's too'.

7
Mr Gladstone's Mission

While this extravaganza was being enacted abroad, there was no lack of sensational events at home. Lincoln's closest friends were pressing Archdeacon Manning or Mr Gladstone to travel out to Italy and bring home the erring sinner. Of lesser magnitude, though sufficiently alarming to warrant a note in the Duke's diary, was the illness of his thirty-five-year-old son, Lord Thomas, in the autumn of 1848. 'Thomas taken ill on the very day that saw Lord George Bentinck a corpse',* ran the entry. Thomas's heart had almost ceased to beat, but the doctor having laid a mustard poultice over it and on the stomach, his patient recovered, and the Duke continued his diary, ascribing the illness to his son having gone to Torquay where the 'relaxing climate with bad vapours' had weakened him. Closing on an optimistic note, he was cheered by the conjecture that it would 'doubtless be for his good in some way we cannot see'.[n]

Nor had the Duke been laggardly, having made a marriage proposal for himself. In December of that year Lady Emily Foley, daughter of the Duke of Montrose, and now for some years a widow, had invited the Duke and his daughters to pay her a visit at Stoke Edith in Herefordshire for the purpose of attending a ball. No doubt this was prompted by kindness for it must have been a matter of general concern to all well-wishers that none of the Ladies Pelham-Clinton were yet married. Lady Georgiana was already thirty-eight and was probably considered beyond marriageable age, but it was unusual for younger sisters to gain suitors if the elder ones had not yet acquired husbands. To the Duke, who had known Lady Emily when her elder sister was the first wife of his old friend the Earl of Winchilsea, she appeared on this occasion a pattern of all womanly virtues. 'She is

---

* He had died very suddenly while at Welbeck and the Duke must have been one of the very first to hear of it. Lord George had fought Peel over the Corn Laws and in consequence had earned the Duke's respect.

admirable & good & agreeable, amiable, virtuous, manners perfect, every external and internal gift but beauty; she is not handsome, but so pleasing that no one can be in her company without delighting in it beyond all powers of description.'[n] They found a large house party and the Duke enjoyed the shooting; on the night of the ball at Hereford 'through Lady Emily's kindness' partners were found for his daughters for every dance. They were not home till past three o'clock in the morning, a piece of dissipation which the Duke noted uncritically in his diary. On December 18th he left 'with a heavy heart'. A letter was sent off immediately from Clumber, conveying something warmer than his thanks for a delightful visit, for on Christmas Eve he 'received a letter which has given me infinite consolation'; his heart was overflowing with gratitude. But on the last day of the year there came, by post, the blighting of 'all my sanguine hopes & expectations. It is a grievous & bitter disappointment to me, the greatest that I ever experienced & I fear that I may not easily get over it.' She had refused his proposal of marriage, and the 'miserable disappointment' was 'bitter in the extreme & near to breaking my heart'. He felt himself to be 'unfortunate & unsuccessful in every undertaking & expectation of my life – this the greatest of all' and on the first day of 1849 he admitted to his diary that the new year appeared 'woefully inauspicious. I feel as if I could never be tranquil again or survive the calamity.' As usual when looking back on the old year the Duke found something to 'astonish him beyond all description', but on this occasion it is we, peeping into his diary, who are astounded to find that to the Duke the year 1848 seemed 'the most extraordinary & eventful year that has occurred since the coming of our Saviour'.[n] The rapid fulfilment of prophecy he found 'most marked & indubitable'. Upheaval in the Church, revolution in France, Chartist movement at home, had indeed marked the old year; also Susan's elopement, but of her there was no mention.

In writing to Suzie at Rome in the autumn of 1848, Mrs Gladstone had suggested what appeared to her a means of avoiding calumny, for she had been unaware of Lord Walpole's presence, but as spring (1849) approached the scandal grew in magnitude, and although no whisper of pregnancy had yet filtered back to England, Suzie's abandonment of any pretension to virtue was notorious. At the beginning of 1849 Lincoln had taken rooms at 16 Carlton House Terrace; his younger children had spent the winter with the Sidney Herberts at

Wilton House, Salisbury, and he was now searching for a little villa for them within easy distance of London. He had not so far been successful, and they were quartered at the Star and Garter, Richmond. He was not well, and missing his wife grievously, and at about the time of Mrs Gladstone's letter to Susan he had written revealingly to his old friend Henry Manning, now Archdeacon of Chichester.

Wilton House,[51]
24 Nov. 1848

My dear Archdeacon Manning, I was gratified at the interpretation you put upon my letter for it was written freely and as the sentiments of the heart occurred to me – and therefore it had, I believe, the merit of sincerity – but I still fear you overrate the effect which deep and constant and long continued, though often varying sorrow, has yet had upon my mind. You speak I fear more of yourself than of me when you say that suffering in silence and solitude makes us leave off resting on anything which can change, and seeking our happiness in anything which is not eternal. Were it so I should cease to mourn for my blighted hopes of domestic happiness, my heart would yearn less after her who has offended me and more after God whom I have offended ... In one thing I do feel that the long continuance of my sorrow has improved the temper of my mind. Formerly I may have felt heated in spirit and resentful when my Wife's conduct brought grief and shame upon me – now I hope and believe it is far otherwise and yet strange it is that I never suffered in spirit so much as now, on no former occasion have I felt so sick at heart or so incapable of comfort. I think, as well as hope, I mourn for her even more than for myself – I know I am indifferent to the scoffs of men and the rebukes of friends when they see that I care for her still – and in one sense at least, that in which I believe forgiveness is enjoined, I have forgiven her already. Why then do I feel a deeper grief now than when sorrow of this deep dye was yet young? I hope it is because on former occasions I buoyed myself with a hope to restore a Mother to my Children – now I despair.

You will not be surprised that the people who are endeavouring to assist me in saving my unhappy Wife from utter destruction if it is yet possible are William Gladstone and his admirable Wife. Of course I cannot appear to be a party to anything that is done but Mrs Gladstone is most kindly and judiciously making a last effort for what alone can now be hoped. God grant that contrary to all human probabilities it may be successful ...

Believe me to be ever, yours sincerely and affectionately

LINCOLN

By March there was a concerted agreement among Lincoln's friends that Susan should be fetched home and made to live with her husband again. At that stage the two most concerned were Sir Robert Peel and Sir Frederick Thesiger, later 1st Lord Chelmsford and Lord Chancellor. 'Take in that *Thesiger* and *Peel* were the two who advised and decided the journey abroad',[52] Lady Lyttelton, a sister of Catherine Gladstone, wrote to her husband. Preliminaries were settled in June: Lincoln's friends had rallied, and Gladstone was informed of 'new & very painful evidence raising for the first time in my mind the serious fear that poor Lady L may have committed the last act of infidelity'.[53] There followed for the next few weeks a comedy of quite devastating proportions – although the participants, Sir Robert Peel, Gladstone, Thesiger, Archdeacon Manning, all men preeminent in their stations, seem not to have viewed their 'Mission' in any light but that of the sternest duty. On July 7th Gladstone re-ported: 'Saw Lincoln & then Peel with him. We talked chiefly on the subject of the Mission. L having said that the only persons he would like to send were in circumstances to render it impossible, I told him he ought to let them judge that. He thereupon named Manning & me, & I undertook to write to M & said it might be impracticable for me – which Catherine approved',[54] she being near her sixth con-finement. That day, marking his letter 'Secret', Gladstone wrote to Manning.

6 Carlton Gardens[55]

July 7th 1849

My dear Manning, I am now going to put a question on my own responsibility alone which will surprise you but you will excuse it on account of my motive, which is to be prepared as far as pos-sible with the best advice in that most painful case of which you have heard from our friend most interested recently, and from time to time. You know what has lately been heard of her equivo-cal and precarious condition, these epithets describing it under its best aspect. I am most deeply desirous that no other question should be entertained at all until every means of stopping evil or averting danger by gentle influences shall have been exhausted. A formal mission from hence to Naples *now and with* despatch is that which suggests itself if it can be arranged. I fear that you may have *more* than *one* insuperable impediment to undertaking alone or in company such a mission, still you are the judge of your own calling, and comparative obligations and therefore I want to know from yourself secretly and speedily whether *such* impediments do or do not exist. I have in mind 1. your health and the probable risk to it from a rapid and therefore laborious journey – 2. your engagements in the Archdeaconery – the call on the other side being I must admit a forlorn hope or something near it. Worst of all would of course be a third impediment that none would be entitled to challenge – but this in your case I do not suppose – as I know you would only entertain the questions of duty and charity.

Now pray distinguish between this letter which I write of my own motion to obtain information, and a request to you – which may never be made and which of course I am not authorized to make … I ought so far to define my own credentials of such a mission as to say that I imagine it would have for its object inducing her to place herself in a position free humanly speaking from danger and affording reasonable guarantees for conduct whether by return to this country, joining friends abroad, or otherwise.

Over recent years Manning had suffered appalling strain. Appointed to the Archdeaconry of Chichester in 1840, his early charges had been deeply concerned with religious unity and discipline, but of late the Anglican Church had been shaken fundamentally by vital issues, which to Manning represented a church in schism. The Jerusalem Bishopric; State involvement in the established religious education of schools; the Hampden controversy; the affair of W. T. Allies; and finally the Gorham Case, all served to weaken a faith already crippled by doubts.* He had been severely ill

---

* The Rev. R. D. Hampden, alleged to hold heterodox views, had been appointed to the See of Hereford; the Rev. W. T. Allies had publicly denounced Anglican dogma; the Rev. G. C. Gorham had openly denied his belief in baptismal regeneration.

in 1847, and with death seemingly close at hand had drawn percep-
tibly nearer to what he claimed to be the 'reality of the Roman ...
Church'.[56] Gladstone, his closest friend, though ignorant of the force
of this conviction, knew something of the peril he was undergoing,
though Manning had preferred to be silent on this one fearful con-
flict, aware of the affection it would destroy.* Manning was powerless at this time to reconcile the contending forces affecting his
conscience with a life dedicated to the cure of souls in the church to
which he had been ordained, though he was already perhaps emo-
tionally treading the path to Rome while still held by his intellect.
Such a letter as this, proposing that this most ascetic of priests should
hasten to Naples without delay (in the heat of the Mediterranean
sun) and there detach an offending wife from the accommodating
arms of her profligate lover, strikes a note so incongruous that Manning's refusal, though gently veiled and generously phrased, had the
merit of presuming that the present predicament was not to be resolved by human agency.

Lavington. July 8, 1849.[57]

My dear Gladstone, Your letter brings me to a question on which
I have as you truly say a ready will. My circumstances are these:

   1. My visitations are not over until the 19th, and although I
could start immediately it would be difficult under some days.

   2. A rapid journey – such as you would make – I am not able to
bear without illness ...

But I dare not say no to such a judgement as your's, and in such
a case: especially as I said some time ago to our Friend that if she
returned to any place nearer England, I would gladly go if he
desired it. My chief fear is health. I am well, thank God, so long as
I can avoid strain and derangement of habit but a slight thing pro-
duces general disturbance ... If it were possible for me my whole
heart and will would be ready. It would be hard to say how I have
entered into their sorrow. Since he first wrote to me I have had it
literally in my thoughts every day.

   All that I can say is that God is over all and will rule all to His

---

* From the day of Manning's apostasy, Gladstone neither saw nor spoke to him again
until twelve years later, when correspondence was resumed.

will. But these are strange exorbitancies; not to be reduced to any order or law till we are above all the course of heaven and earth. The manly and great sorrow of our friend is an example, and makes me feel not only affection for him.

Let me hear from you again. Ever yours affectionately,

H.E. MANNING

Further meetings resulted, Gladstone offering to go himself to Naples, his wife having urged on him the duty of doing so – she would have gone with him, had she not been so near her confinement. Manning sent additional moral assistance.

Lavington, July 12th 1849[58]

My dear Gladstone, ... I need not say to you how I feel that you have advised and done the best thing and in the best of ways. May you have your fullest reward in restoring a wife to herself and then to her home. I know of no act of your life that would fill you with such joy at the last. In what way can I join with you? My visitation is a public obligation from which I could not withdraw myself without real failure to duty, and probable harm to others. In this I am not free to choose. But after this is done I will hold myself ready to come and meet you or to assist in any way which will forward the objects of your mission. We cannot say beforehand whether this will be needful or not: but I wish you to know that I will answer your call, God willing.

May you be kept safely and may your home be in peace till you come back. Believe me, Ever your affectionate friend,

H.E. MANNING

On July 11th: 'Attended at Peel's in the forenoon' (Gladstone, in his diary, reckoned it 'a great privilege to be able to call in his aid') 'where it has been decided to accept my offer to go to Naples. So I had to commence my preparations forthwith.'[59] On the night of the 13th he was on his way, carrying in his pocket a letter from his wife to Suzie. He had also found time that day to see Lincoln once more and to write to Manning.

Secret

6 Carlton Gardens, July 13th 1849[60]

My dear Manning, I write in great haste on the point of starting by to-night's Mail Train ... I deeply feel how much better L would have been served, and she also, had it been in your power to have gone at once with safety, but I think Lincoln felt that so long a journey at the present season could not be warrantably undertaken by you under circumstances of any pressure ... Should the Mission be so far prospered as to bring her within reach, morally and locally, I think L will be very anxious to call your generous offer into life.

Gladstone crossed the Channel in the early hours of the 14th and, having been 'sick enough', reached Paris during the course of the morning. His hope was to perform his task with the utmost zeal and return to his wife as fast as possible. In Paris, where he had not been since the revolution of 1848, he found that the manager of the Hotel Bristol did not scruple to express hopes for '"quelque changement politique", which I fancy meant a restoration, but the difficulty is which of the rival exiles to bring back? It is ludicrous to see "Liberté, Egalité, Fraternité" painted everywhere & to know that it is not worth the price of the paint used in putting it up.'[61] Writing to 'My beloved Cathie' from Marseilles on July 17th he lamented that he would be unable to accomplish the journey to Naples as fast as he had hoped. 'The case I find stands thus. The boat that should have sailed from hence today, called Il Lombardo, was detained it seems at Genoa on account of its having on board Mazzini and Saffi, two of the Roman triumvirs * and some question as to whether they could land ... which I cannot understand, particularly as Armellini, the third of them, is now here, and is I am told in this hotel [Beauveau] itself; one of the Hotel people tells me he is extremely little and ugly. Possibly I may send in my card and try to see him but I must avoid anything that would cause me to be taken for a politician, I mean a Continental one.'[62] Meanwhile he had time on his hands and employed some of his leisure in reading Lincoln's letters to Manning. (The exchange of letters seems to have been very much common practice and no resentment was displayed at letters being circulated amongst friends. The entire seriousness with which they were submitted and analysed probably redeemed the writer from any embarrassment.) Gladstone considered that they threw light upon the character of Lincoln's mind 'which has been I think in a wonderful

---

* In the Italian war of liberation.

manner both deepened & expanded by his sorrows. They are noble and beautiful letters & I am greatly rejoiced to have them with me for they cannot fail to strengthen my hands which are indeed but too weak in every way.'[63] He was also concerned with what his attitude towards Lord Walpole should be, 'for if I find her in habits of social intercourse with *him* I must decline meeting *him*, it seems to me, at all events until after her decision shall have been taken in the sense that we wish. It is not that *I* am entitled to refuse intercourse with him on general grounds, but that it would be incompatible in honour with that which I have to say and do concerning him. Thus far have I gone in my meditations as to preliminaries.'[64] While occupied with reflections of an ethical nature, his sensibilities were affected in another fashion. He found the *'smells* – I use the mildest term because the strongest would be infinitely too weak' worse in Marseilles in high summer weather than in Paris: 'where they were vile, here they are the superlative of everything. The Port runs up into the very heart of the town. All its filth is discharged there, and lies perfectly stagnant so that the mass of water is blacker than you would ever see the filthiest little puddle in England.' He prepared his wife for worse: 'The odiferous streams run through the open streets, but now comes the climax which will strain your powers of belief: men, women & children are busy with a kind of large wooden spoon projecting this stuff out of gutters all over the streets by way of watering them!'[65] He was thankful to leave Marseilles at last, and though there was 'motion' on board, the journey was comfortable enough, in signal contrast to the night crossing from Genoa to Leghorn, where he arrived 'rather battered', having survived the 'roughest night I have been out in'; he lay down on deck till midnight while the crew staggered or crawled about as best they could. At Rome he found his way to Serni's not, as one might conclude, on Walpole's trail, but for 'draughts of tea' which he enjoyed exceedingly. He reached Naples on the morning of July 24th having driven post during the night, with only a stop at Capua for customs, and ices for refreshment. He put up at the Crocelle, a large hotel commanding a view over part of the bay, familiar to him from his earlier visit in 1838, for here, as he reminded Catherine the next day,[66] 'this place, this house, & on this day, is full of its own associations. I feel myself to be beneath the roof where near 12 years ago when Kinnaird & I could not get our bell answered at dinner we were told it was because *una grande famiglia*

Inglese had just arrived & put the house in confusion – it was yours, & you had been guided hither to bless my life.'* It was not long however before he discovered that the culmination of his journey had not yet been gained, and that Susan had moved north. 'I must now I fear', he continued, 'entirely abandon the idea which I had cherished that I might be able to stay long enough to see her move out of the way of extreme danger – and again if I have the opportunity to act at all it will now be necessary for me to act with more rapidity. But you must not suppose that the new chase which I have to begin in the least alters my ideas as to the time when I should come home ... I am as much convinced as ever it was right to make the attempt, and I never repent of having come whatever deep misgivings I feel of my own fitness for the work.'[67] During the best part of three days Gladstone was occupied with his letters to Lincoln, to his banker, to his wife; he made enquiries of William Temple, the Minister, and the attaché, Lionel Sackville-West; he also questioned Mme Unghara, who he later believed had been aware of Susan's condition. He managed with 'great speed' to get to Sorrento – 'more like Paradise than common earth' – and was at last on his way to Milan, 'and then my prospects of finding must get either better or worse'. From Genoa, having collected a courier, Gladstone, describing it as a 'hot & dusty journey until sunset across the Appenines', reached Milan the next morning. 'I found myself in one of the best Inns anywhere at breakfast with luxuries on my right hand & on my left i.e. ice to my butter to keep it cold & flaming spirits of wine to my head to keep it hot.'[68] Later that evening, continuing his letter, Gladstone unfolded the events of the day.

> I had to set about finding Lady L with no other knowledge than (what afterwards proved to be false namely) that she was somewhere in the city on the 21st. After examining the book of the hotel (La Citta) without any success, I determined to go to headquarters, the Police itself, & I found the official people most courteous: but judge of my perplexity when I could not find her name at all! I then bethought myself that L had told me she sometimes

* The associations were indeed memorable. It was nearly eleven years (not twelve) since Gladstone had travelled in Italy with A. F. Kinnaird (later 10th Baron, now M.P. for Perth), and was staying at the hotel when the Glynne family arrived. Gladstone and Catherine were married on July 25th (the following year), the date of this letter.

made use of another half foreign name in travelling such as
Lefevre or Latouche, & without giving a name at all asked to look
through all the Ls who had been in Milan – but I could find nothing, & my hopes had sunk very low indeed at this point when I
asked if the police could give me any further aid, & was told in
reply *No* … I had furnished myself with a letter from Unghara of
Naples to a friend of his who keeps a neat Inn here so I went to
him: but no name in his book could have been Lady L and I left
his house determined to search all the considerable Inns, and not
by the proper name only, but by carefully examining the books &
making enquiries as to appearance which might guide me. So I
went to six of them in all & the wheel turned round again: first of
all I met an old man who was confident he had seen some such
person and at last at the Gran Bretagna I found that a person had
been there under the name of Mrs Laurence who was a *signora
Inglese* travelling with only a courier & a maid. So I asked about
her appearance – 'Era bella assai benché lo stata ammalata?' 'Si,
era specialmente una assai bella figura.' 'Cappelli neri?' 'Si.'
'Occhi neri?' 'Si.' 'Bocca un po aperta?' 'Si.'* So now my hopes
were quite up again. But on proceeding to gather all the rest of the
information that I could, I found that … she had a courier named
Santi; her passport was taken for England via Switzerland but the
courier said they were going to Como & were *then to take some
place upon the lake,* and someone had since told the landlord that
this had actually been done! I then went back to the Police, found
the name of Laurence but without anything to mark whether man
or woman. The maid's name entered 'Williams', also the Courier
with a name different from that which the landlord knew to be his
proper one. Lastly I found from the landlord that the woman was
English and, as he said, *bellagiovanni* [a fine young woman] which
I cannot answer as I never saw Mrs Job. However I am sanguine
all things considered that this must be Lady L – and pretty clear
on the other hand that if it be not, I can hardly prosecute the
search further here. Accordingly I go tomorrow by daybreak and
from thence up the lake as I may be directed. But now comes
another point – Lord W. I find he came to Milan straight from

* Loosely translated: 'Though ill, still beautiful?' 'Yes, she was outstandingly handsome.' 'Dark hair and eyes.' 'The mouth slightly open?' 'Yes.'

Genoa – went on the next day – took his passport in the same terms as Lady L – but I find from what his courier said that he went towards Chiavenna at the *North* end of the Lake of Como. I also learnt that he had no lady with him. From these circumstances it seems not certain but far from improbable that they are together or near one another on the Lake of Como. But at any rate a day or two I trust will bring all this out. & now I close for this evening.[69]

He had still energy for an evening at the opera, and after three hours' sleep (though even this was 'bitten away') was called at three-thirty in the morning, and not neglecting a fifteen-minute visit to the Duomo, was off to Como an hour later.

At home Lady Lyttelton, who was staying in London to be with her sister during Gladstone's absence, thought the campaign of coaxing Suzie home an absurd one, and on August 3rd wrote to her husband: 'I do think it is an insane plan, tho' William writes in a grand heroic strain as if great purposes were to be achieved.'[70] But on that very day he had already turned his face towards home, defeated in his 'great purpose', if confident of its ultimate good. 'But all the … cares are suppressed by the deadly weight of the subject which I carried out with me', he wrote in his diary, '& now in a far more aggravated form I carry home. I have but one real comfort: a hope flows in upon me, nay a belief, founded perhaps on the worthlessness & brutality of the seducer in this case, that the day of penitence will come, & that then this journey, though for no worthiness God knows of mine, may have its fruits.'[71]

The Countess of Lincoln, 1843, from a portrait by James Swinton,
now at Brodick Castle, Isle of Arran.
Reproduced by courtesy of the National Trust for Scotland

The 4th Duke of Newcastle, KG, from a portrait by H. W. Pickersgill, RA.
Reproduced by courtesy of the Palace of Westminster

The Earl of Lincoln, 1848, from a portrait by F. R. Say.
Reproduced by permission of the National Portrait Gallery

Portrait of the 10th Duke of Hamilton by Sir Daniel MacNee.
Reproduced by courtesy of the Scottish National Portrait Gallery

8
Discovery and Flight

Suzie, settling herself at the Villa Mancini* on June 17th, 1849, delighted in her countrified retreat. The house stood opposite the town of Como on the bank of the lake, the high-walled garden stretching down towards its edge, and a little garden gate giving access across the pebbled shore to the water itself. In the front another garden forming a courtyard lay between the house and the principal, heavy iron gates, which when opened allowed a view of the villa from the main road. Walpole joined her there a few days later and his first action was to engage a valet. Giuseppe Trincavelli was recommended by the landlord of the local Albergo del'Angelo. Born at Como thirty years earlier, Trincavelli had been taken as a boy to England, and was soon apprenticed to the looking-glass trade. He worked at Newcastle-upon-Tyne for some years, and on his return to Como, helped by his knowledge of English, secured the job of valet and interpreter to the hotel visitors. On the day of his interview at the villa he met Job (Madame Williams) and Santi, but not until the second day was he aware that there was a woman in the house, Madame Laurence, 'his Lordship's sister'. He described her as handsome, very tall, fair-complexioned, nearing thirty years of age,† and 'quite large, in the family way'. Walpole instructed him in his duties, which were to wait exclusively upon his lordship in his bedroom: in the morning to prepare his shower ('a bath like rain dropping over him'), and make his bed, take up his hot water at night, and assist him in his dressing. When Trincavelli asked how long his service would be required, since it would make a difference in the rate of wages, he was told eight days or a fortnight, or perhaps a month.

The hot July days passed agreeably and uneventfully. Walpole would rise early and walk in the garden. At nine Suzie joined him in the large ground floor salon where they breakfasted together. The

---

* Demolished in 1962 and replaced by an unsightly block of flats.
† She was just thirty-five years of age.

whole morning was spent idling in the garden, usually on a garden seat, reading aloud to each other, laughing and talking. Twice a day Trincavelli went in to Como to collect whatever letters there might be for the household; occasionally on his return he found Suzie and Walpole in the drawing-room by the tall windows, with Suzie lying on the sofa 'and his Lordship sitting on the sofa close to her, not at her feet, but middle way between that and her head'. At half-past two or three they dined, and in the cool of the late afternoon a hired rowing-boat was brought to the little gate. Accompanied only by the boatman, they would remain on the lake until eight or nine. Immediately on their return Walpole changed into the familiar dressing-gown and slippers and tea would follow. He would smoke his cigar and call for fresh water for his favourite drink of gum and water.* By eleven they went upstairs to their rooms; Suzie's was on the first floor, his on the second, but he would linger with her for two hours, or longer. On his fifth night at the villa, Trincavelli got into severe trouble for falling asleep and not being about at four o'clock in the morning when Walpole came up to his room and was himself obliged to waken his valet. He cursed at him in French and 'knocked his feet down on the floor', until Trincavelli explained that he had supposed his master to have dropped asleep on the sofa in his sister's room. Walpole agreed heartily; this was precisely what had occurred, but bade him knock on the door if it should happen again. A few nights later under the same circumstances Trincavelli went to Suzie's door, and knocked. He had first taken the jug of hot water downstairs to reheat at the kitchen fire, and had placed it on the hob to keep warm. It was four o'clock, and having knocked, each time a little louder, he heard two voices, Walpole's calling out 'Vengo'. By now Trincavelli could not have failed to realize that 'they were very fond in their manner and Alessandro (the gardener) and he would laugh together and say: 'It was very kind† Brother and Sister.'

The lovers seemed unsure of the expected date of their child's birth. Walpole's uncertainty when engaging his valet was evident though it seemed to indicate an early confinement; but whether in

---

* Perhaps a solution of gum-arabic, taken in water.
† Trincavelli's English was good, but 'kind' (*dolce, tenero, affezionato*) would be more correctly rendered as 'loving' or 'affectionate'.

eight days or a month, it was probable that he would take his departure as soon afterwards as possible. Susan's powers of attraction
must have been great, for they had been constantly together for
nearly a year, and Walpole was known to tire quickly of every con-
quest. And then, unexpectedly, in the early evening, in the first days
of July, Susan imagined herself in labour. Dottore Balzarri, reluctant
to assist for fear of being out after curfew,* attended her, also a mid-
wife. Although it was a false alarm, Walpole never left the house for
several days. Since nothing was prepared, a young seamstress,
Guiseppina, was engaged for a week or two to make baby clothes
and linen, Job exhorting her constantly to make haste as the baby's
birth was expected shortly.

For a few weeks life at the villa regained its idyllic charm. The great
heat had struck, and the shade of the garden and an occasional breeze
from the water were welcome refreshment from the sun's attentions.
The evening excursions on the lake were revived, and at the end of
July it was when Suzie and Walpole had walked slowly up from the
water in the late evening that they found appalling news awaiting
them at the house. Lord Lincoln would be amongst them directly.

Trincavelli had been at Como for the afternoon letters and had
returned with only one and that for Suzie (presumably from the servant at the Gran Bretagna), informing her that an Englishman had
been making enquiries that morning and would soon be on his way
to Como. To the guilty lovers the Englishman could be no other than
the forsaken husband. Their first impulse was to organize their flight,
and Walpole, not pausing to see Suzie and the servants on their road,
and perhaps eager to escape a situation which was proving an
encumbrance, elected to be off before daylight to Varenna, towards
the top of the lake. The household was in confusion, and Trincavelli,
on receiving orders for a rowboat to be ready at two o'clock in the
morning, enquired of Job and Santi the cause of the disturbance and
was told that the letter had brought an account of the illness of Mrs
Laurence's mother; that they must pack up and go directly if she
wished to see her mother once more alive. Where they were to go
was not revealed – nor any further pretension made to its being Lord
Walpole's mother also. The valet had seen nothing of Suzie, and little

* These were troublesome times in northern Italy, with Venice resisting Austrian dom-
ination.

of his master, until at half-past one Lord Walpole came upstairs and
spent the next hour writing letters. Trincavelli packed, prepared
some coffee, and Walpole left by boat at three, giving him forty
francs with which to pay the washerwoman and his chemist's bill,
and bidding him to go to the police for his passport later in the morning, and to bring it to him at the Hotel de la Poste, Varenna.

When Mr Gladstone reached Como on July 31st, shortly after
Lord Walpole had left it, he breakfasted, and then 'set about the sad
purpose' of his visit, but 'somehow thinking Lord W was not here
and feeling certain I should find Lady L I was light-headed when I
commenced my enquiries'.[72] Learning from the police that Mrs Laurence lived at the Villa Mancini, he presented himself at the iron gate
and sent in his card, handing it to the gardener's wife. She passed it
on to Trincavelli who happened to be at hand and he carried it inside,
giving it to Santi who took it upstairs to Suzie's room where he and
Job were packing. The relief to Suzie must have been overwhelming.
Instead of a husband on the doorstep, legally empowered to drag her
back to England, here was Mr Gladstone whom she could refuse to
see, and might elude during the night. She had probably little inclination to reason out the possibility of his following her, nor the
strength, in the stifling heat, to form any other plan than that which
had been concocted the previous night. The fact that she had been
discovered after a year of reckless irresponsibility, and at the critical
moment of impending confinement, was quite horrifying enough.
She sent Santi down to the gate; Gladstone asked for Mrs Laurence
and was told he could not see her; on enquiring 'in a rather marked
manner' for the Countess of Lincoln, he was assured that no such
person lived there.

It was now vitally important for Gladstone to ascertain the identity
of Mrs Laurence, so settling himself in the courier's room, he
addressed her a letter explaining that if she would allow him an interview he could account for the strangeness of his behaviour. With this
letter (of which he made a copy) he enclosed that of his wife, brought
with him from England, which dwelt upon her affection for Suzie and
gave a pathetic little description of the Lincolns' ten-year-old daughter, Susan. 'I am pleased to show you proofs of the *reality* of our affection,' she wrote. 'Thankful that my Husband can make up his mind to
the sacrifice & anxiety of leaving me just now ... Oh! may the
Christian and tender spirit, the earnest desire which so fills his heart

... produce an effect upon you dear Suzie ... Listen then to that per-
suasive voice which you have so often told me you liked to hear ...
Had it been possible for me to have gone with him to you how quickly
would I have done so. He will tell you how much your dear children
are with us, how deeply affecting it is to see them motherless, but not
by the hand of God. It was only lately that Susan, upon your birthday,
was heard crying in her little bed; alone, as she thought herself, she
cried "Oh Mammy, Mammy, why did you leave us"! She will turn
pale if asked by an unconscious child where her Mama is – she loves
to dwell upon Mammy's singing, Mammy's looks. I think her greatly
improved & her warm heart is full of pretty attentions to the only
Parent that remains, With *him* care & sorrow sits upon his brow.' She
had heard with regret of Suzie's 'tumble' in Rome (the euphemism
given for seclusion when pregnancy became too apparent), and with
true ingenuousness hoped to hear of a happy recovery. 'Ere you read
this', she concluded, 'you will have taken in the rapidity of my dear
William's journey in all this *intense* heat for no other purpose than to
help you ... you will see as much as you can of him & *take care of him
for me*.'[73] In his letter to Catherine that evening Gladstone disclosed
the one great overwhelming shock he had sustained in the knowledge
of Susan's condition, and admitted that learning 'this horror from the
laquais de place who conducted me to the Villa, it threw me into such
a tremor and palpitation that I could hardly write: for I am one of
those who are always sufficiently shocked at other people's sins.'[74]

Trincavelli was called to bring a candle for Gladstone to seal the
letter which Santi then took with him. Gladstone's hope was that in
writing to Mrs Laurence he was providing against the chance of his
being mistaken, which 'morally, I felt sure I was not', while 'Lady
Lincoln's desire to know something about her children might induce
her to open the letter. I think I gave an intimation to that effect to the
courier.'[75] After ten minutes Santi returned with the letter from Mrs
Gladstone, unopened, and a verbal message to the effect that Lady
Lincoln was unknown to Mrs Laurence who could not see him on
grounds of illness.

Returning to the hotel – for it was now afternoon – Gladstone,
having failed to collect evidence of identity, felt obliged to write once
again and was under the illusion that, by requesting, he would obtain
a written reply and thereby recognize Suzie's handwriting. In this he
was no luckier than in his earlier attempt.

Trincavelli meanwhile had not forgotten to fetch his master's passport from the police, where it had been given a visa for Switzerland. His next errand was to order three post horses to be sent up to the villa in the evening, and shortly before their arrival, while standing near the house, he saw to his surprise 'the English Gentleman' walking up and down the road before the gates. By the time the horses arrived and had entered the front court it was quite dark and Trincavelli lowered the lantern over the front door and lit it so that the carriage could be packed with the greatest speed. Gladstone meanwhile passed and repassed the gates. Santi came out of the house and handed Trincavelli a packet of letters addressed to Walpole to be given to him with his passport the next day, cautioning him that should the English Gentleman be also going to Varenna on the same boat, he must be sure to reach Lord Walpole first and warn him.

Everything was now ready for a stealthy departure; the packing had been accomplished so quickly that five minutes only had elapsed since the arrival of the carriage. In silence Suzie and Job came downstairs to the door, wearing cloaks, bonnets, and heavy veiling. As they stood for an instant under the lantern near the carriage, as if waiting to enter it, Gladstone noted a figure wrapped in a cloak which he seemed to recognize as that of Susan. At the same moment Santi, looking about him as though to make sure no one was on the watch, observed the lamp over the door and cursed Trincavelli for having lighted it and bade him put it out. Without taking leave of Trincavelli, and in total silence, the two women climbed into the carriage while Santi got up behind. As the carriage passed through the gates, Gladstone, standing on tiptoe ('he raised himself up a little'), attempted to see inside, but the blinds were down. He had not dared to go into the courtyard at the moment of departure to satisfy himself of the identity of the heavily veiled woman, for 'weighing all things, and putting all things together, and the extreme undesirableness, from what I believed of the state of Lady Lincoln, of my appearing suddenly before her, I desisted'. The carriage drove towards Lecco on the road to Verona, while Gladstone, exhausted from shock and distress, wrote to his wife.

Oh my Cathie, I am now sorely cast down & sick at heart in this other earthly paradise to which people come for deeds of hell. I am not certain – I may be wrong. Mrs Laurence & Lady Lincoln may be different persons – there are points in which the descriptions are not complete and clear. I have no *demonstration* either of eye or ear – but alas! of *this* there is no doubt whatever, the Mrs Laurence as she is called who refused two times over to see or communicate with me except by verbal message today, & who drove off from her Villa between nine & ten tonight with closed blinds, is *far gone in pregnancy!* It is heartbreaking: but with what joy shall I go down on my knees before her to ask her pardon if, what an if, Mrs Laurence is not Lady L. I do not know how I ought to feel under the great shock of seeming discovery of this terrible calamity. There may be hopes it is a dream.

Too tired to write more, he yet could grieve for the 'triumph of hellish wickedness over a woman of the rarest gifts, and the utter devastation of heart & home & profanation of the holy mystery of marriage. Lord have mercy upon us, Christ have mercy upon us, Lord have mercy upon us.'[76]

He was up early the next morning, going first in search of Dr Balzarri who had attended Suzie. Not finding him, he caught the eight o'clock steamer to Varenna to make enquiries about Lord Walpole. The contrast between the 'rapid voyage [3½ hours], sweet & cool air upon the lake, with its beautiful scenery & sky, and the business I was about' he found truly horrible.[77] Apparently he had not recognized Trincavelli, also on board, who ran directly to the hotel to acquaint his master with the news. Walpole, much put out, desired him to go first to the innkeeper and tell him that if his name was in the visitors' book to scratch it out, and then to go about the town and discover the English Gentleman's movements. Gladstone, receiving no information at the hotel, hired a carriage and drove the twelve miles to Lecco to seek out Suzie. Trincavelli, seeing him drive by and learning his direction at the Grande Place, also hired a carriage, and hurried after. Finding that Susan had driven on to Bergamo the previous night, Gladstone could follow no further, so, sleeping at Lecco, he returned to Como the next day, August 2nd, collected his belongings and made his departure for Milan, and from thence to England. Depressed and saddened beyond measure, travelling all night from Brig, he reached Lausanne at midday on Sunday, and 'finding there was H.C.' he went 'unwashed & unshorn to the Service', later in the day writing in his diary: 'Oh that poor miserable Lady L – once the dream of dreams, the image that to my young eye combined every thing that earth could offer of beauty and of joy. What is she now! But may that Spotless Sacrifice whereof I partook, unworthy as I am, today avail for her, to the washing away of sin, & to the renewal of the image of God.'[78]

Almost his first act on reaching home was to write to Manning.

Secret

6 C[arlton] G[ardens] August 10th 1849[79]
My dear Manning, I came home at eleven last night, after a journey of which the labours, the interest, and the anxieties, all great, alike vanish into utter insignificance when compared with the afflicting weight of the circumstances it has revealed to me ... You will be shocked and stunned to hear that I can entertain no moral doubt whatever of the fact that the unhappy subject of our cares is within a few weeks, probably a few days of her delivery – this tells all ... The case is beyond reasonable doubt in my view: and I conceive it to be immoral in a husband to allow such matter to remain beyond the notice of the law. There will, I cannot doubt, be a suit of divorce.

Unable to discover Gladstone at Lecco, Trincavelli had immediately driven back to Como, and the following day, August 2nd, on arriving at Varenna, found Lord Walpole in bed complaining of illness; so Trincavelli was sent off to Menaggio, three miles away, to fetch a doctor. He carried back sixteen leeches 'for to put on His Lordship'; a bottle of the favourite gum from Como, stockings, and 'half stockings' were the next errands. He was paid his wages and left Walpole's service with instructions to the Post Office to redirect any letters for the party to the 'Rhino Germanico'. Walpole had expressed no desire to have news of Suzie, who for her part on that day, August 2nd, while her lover at Varenna was lamenting his health and Gladstone was packing his bag at Como, gave birth to a son at the Hotel Torre de Londra, Verona.

Suzie had reached there with little time to spare. Unkind fate in the guise of Mr Gladstone had displaced Lord Walpole, but she still had with her the courier Santi, her maid, and the travelling carriage, and on arriving at Verona in the afternoon of August 1st, the hall porter, in the absence at Monza of the hotel keeper, accommodated them with the best apartments. The hotel, small but good, with an arched portico supported by two columns ('resembling that in the Strand on the north side of St. Clement Dane's Church leading to Staple Inn'),* faced the Corso Sta Anastasia; at the back, with a small gallery running round it, lay a courtyard. The principal rooms on the first floor, those occupied by Suzie, were a few feet from the staircase landing, and looked out to the front: her *'grand salon'*, as the hotel called it, had two windows and a balcony, a bedroom next door, and a smaller room behind it. She was delivered the next morning, a year and a day since her escape from bondage, and later when information for the divorce was collected from the staff, there was nothing to suggest it had been an awkward delivery. Her traumatic experiences of the last forty-eight hours may have brought forward the birth, but, as in the case of earlier confinements, she stood it well and was in no danger. The baby was baptized Horatio on August 25th in Suzie's sitting-room, Santi and Signor Erbatte, the landlord, standing as godfathers. The certificate of baptism was made out by the Reverendo Angelo Ganassini on a loose sheet of paper instead of in the Parish Register (this being accounted for by the child not having been presented in the Church, according to its usages, either by the father or mother), and the parents' names inscribed as Horatio Walpole Laurent, and Harriet – no further name for her being given. (It seemed to Gladstone, hearing later 'of the name given to the child & the names recorded for the parents', that they had been 'dictated by nothing less than infatuation'.)

In England a few days later, Mr Henderson, the Duke of Newcastle's solicitor, wrote to acquaint him with the recent circumstances. Information had been supplied by Mr Parkinson, Lincoln's solicitor, since Lincoln and his father were not on terms. The Duke resorted to his diary to unburden his mind. 'I have written at some length to Henderson with particulars of how he should advise Mr Parkinson to proceed so that Ly L's infamy shall be completely proved & exposed, & that this little bastard shall not be palmed upon my family as a legitimate child & a Clinton. It is a most scandalous & horrible affair, but is no more than I expected & foretold of Ly L when Lincoln so weakly & inconceivably took her back when she took him by storm at Ryde.' And a few days later: 'Everything has

* Probably Temple Bar, the large stone arched gateway by Wren to the east of the church, but near Chancery Lane which ran north to Staple Inn (an Inn of Chancery).

been done to bring Lady Lincoln's filthy wickedness to light and probably a divorce may follow as well as illegitimizing the bastard.'[11] But for a divorce to take place, for which an Act of Parliament was required, proof more absolute than Mr Gladstone's revelations had to be supplied. The cardinal issue, to be ascertained beyond all doubt, was whether Lady Lincoln and Mrs Laurence were one and the same, and only someone familiar with Susan's appearance could be relied upon.

Joseph Asman, aged thirty, of Ponsonby Terrace, Millbank, for eight years butler in the Lincoln household (who had accompanied his master to Ryde at the time Suzie was posting to Ems), and previous to that fourteen months as footman to the Duke, was selected to go abroad in the company of a Mr Lewis Raphael, of about the same age, solicitor in Bedford Row, a frequent traveller, fluent in Italian and French, but who had never set eyes on Suzie. The two men set off on August 28th, Asman acting as servant to Raphael, who found him 'well educated and well conducted'. Como was the first destination, and from there they followed reports of Susan's easily identifiable party on to Bergamo and Brescia: Santi's appearance seemed memorable. Raphael was told they had headed for the Tyrol, but on enquiring for rooms in Verona at the Torre de Londra at two o'clock in the morning, he was informed that the best beds, those on the first floor, were not available, an English family being in occupation. They accepted rooms on the second floor, and Raphael's suspicions were doubly aroused on hearing a baby crying during the night in the room beneath him. In the morning, looking down on the balcony below, he saw a nurse with an infant in long clothes in her arms ('quite a young thing'), and beckoned to Asman to witness the incident. On enquiring of the waiter where the crying came from he was told from the rooms of 'mi lady inglese', and meeting the nurse on the landing carrying the child, Raphael remarked in Italian: 'A little fellow-countryman of mine', to which she replied that the child was a genuine local, though its mother was English. For fear that Asman might be prematurely recognized by Suzie, he was sent off to kick his heels in Padua and then in Venice, while Raphael did some further reconnoitring. From descriptions he was able to recognize Santi, and Job ('always dressed in silks'), and the travelling carriage. But it was not till he had been there ten days that he caught his first sight of Suzie going for an airing at three o'clock in the afternoon, leaning on the landlord's arm, and seemingly less weak than he had been led to expect. The hotel carriage stood under the portico, and once Suzie had placed herself, Job, carrying shawls over her arm, sat down beside her. The landlord joined them, also a birdcage-maker who lived opposite the hotel and acted as *cicerone* or *valet de place* on occasions. Suzie attracted a good deal of attention at this first outing since her confinement, and it was plain to Raphael that throughout the hotel there was an attempt at concealment, for none of the waiters, nor Luigi, the barber who lived on the ground floor of the hotel on the left of the entrance, nor yet the coffee-house keeper who occupied a shop on the opposite side of the hotel, knew her by any other name than 'Milady inglese'. Later, in conversation with Scavani, the second waiter, Raphael discovered that Suzie would soon be leaving for Florence, so the next day he fetched Asman from Venice, and they returned to Verona on September 18th. They moved their rooms to the entresol so that Asman should not be seen going up and down stairs, yet anyone coming down must pass their doors. Two days later, in the afternoon, Raphael noticed a barouche being prepared for Suzie, so he stationed Asman in a passage which was dark and concealed him from view, though Suzie, passing within a few yards, could be clearly seen, slowly descending the staircase. 'That's her! That's her Ladyship!' Asman exclaimed. The maid followed immediately after and he again burst out with 'That's Job!' His manner on recognizing Suzie and little Arthur's wet-nurse was so genuine that Raphael was convinced they were the persons he claimed.

Two days later (September 22nd), Raphael, having procured the child's baptism certificate from the officiating priest, was at the Police Station making enquiries as to particulars of Suzie's arrival in Verona, when he learned that on that very morning she had obtained a visa for Bologna by way of Mantua. Hurrying back to the hotel he saw Santi packing the travelling carriage in the courtyard and Job going back and forth with packages. Raphael detected an endeavour to conceal their departure from him, and even the waiters kept out of his way. He then wrote Asman's name on one of his own visiting-cards, and calling the landlord, desired him to take it up to the Countess of Lincoln's apartments. Signor Erbatte professed to know of no such person. Raphael told him bluntly that he knew well enough, 'though perhaps I knew more about her than he did', adding that he would ruin his hotel 'if he took ladies in to give birth to children on the sly'. The landlord protested that he had been at Monza when she arrived, but nevertheless he carried up Raphael's card in double quick time. Presently Santi came downstairs and spoke to Raphael, who turning to Asman told him that 'Mrs Job refuses to see you', at the same time explaining to Santi that Asman was 'the former Butler to the Countess of Lincoln'. Asman, he said, was delighted to see her looking so well. Upon this Asman spoke up to the effect that he thought her looking very pale, but not so ill as he expected – hoping to indicate that he knew of her confinement. He expressed a wish 'to see Mrs Job my old fellow servant, and also to pay my duty to my Lady, if her Ladyship would like to see me'. Muttering that he knew his mistress only as Mrs Laurence, Santi withdrew, and Raphael and Asman disposed themselves by the stairs to watch Suzie pass as she took her departure. To their provocation she managed to dodge them by reaching the courtyard from the surrounding gallery; hearing the sound of wheels they ran to the window and watched the carriage under the broiling afternoon sun bowling jauntily along the dusty cobbled street taking the direction of the Mantua road, Suzie inside merrily preparing for some new adventure, and Santi up on the rumble.

9

The Earl of Lincoln's Divorce

Mr Gladstone's return to England in August had brought Lincoln to London. Their first meeting, at which Sir Frederic Thesiger and Mr Parkinson joined them, was related purely to divorce proceedings, to which Lincoln, feeling 'like a Man on his way to the scaffold', had now become resigned as inevitable. After his departure Gladstone chronicled in his diary 'one noble thing he said that I must not let fall to the ground: "I hope the time may come when I may be able to revenge myself on her by some act of kindness done to her without her knowledge" ... Here is a spirit deeply Christian governing all his movements towards her.'[80] Sir Robert Peel had written his deep concern to hear the result of that mission which, with unparalleled kindness and generosity you undertook in the hope of ... conducing possibly to the salvation of a wife and mother ... I can offer you nothing in return for that which you undertook with the promptitude of affectionate friendship ... but that of my sincere admiration for truly virtuous and generous conduct.'[81] But Gladstone, who eight years later opposed the Divorce Bill in the House of Commons, yet who recognized it as a necessity with regard to Lincoln, could not reconcile such a step on ecclesiastical or legislative grounds, and addressed himself to Manning for advice.[82]

> ... But what divorce? a Church divorce only? or a Parliamentary divorce or both? A Church divorce does not dissolve the *vinculum matrimonii* – does not (I suppose) touch in its essence the mystical union of man and wife. A Parliamentary divorce purports to do this inasmuch as it sets the parties free to marry again. Two things perplex me here. One, if the apparent sense of Scripture be the real one, I do not know why the law of the Church absolutely refuses divorce *a circulo*. I rather conjecture the case to be, that this was revived for dispensation in each particular case: that with us the machinery for dispensation dropped: & that being with justice regarded as practically corrupt it has not been revived. A secular

agency has taken its place – and here arises my second difficulty. I cannot understand how all the acts of Parliament in the Universe can *touch* the mystical union of one man to one woman. I know not *if* there be, according to the true will of God, a real dissolution of that union – and if there be, it seems as if there were no other real organ of law in *that* respect than the private conscience ...

In reply Manning emphasized the argument against re-marriage, a contingency that Lincoln's friends must surely have anticipated as a happy issue out of all his afflictions.

Private

London, Sept 3 1849[83]

My dear Gladstone ... The subject of your last letter has hardly been out of my mind since I received it ... There is no doubt that the bond of matrimony is indissoluble by the law of England based upon the law of the Western Church. The Parliamentary licences to marry again are 'privilegia' exempting the individuals from the penalties of the general law. I know that Bishop Cosin and men of high standing in his day, when the first privilegia was granted, argued for the dissolubleness of marriage at least on one ground. And the Greek Church seems to have permitted it. But my inclinations are to abide by our law, and to wish that the privilegia were not granted or sought. A Church divorce ... is obviously a duty in this most mournful case ... Thus far there can be no question.

If I should say what I should most desire for one who has been afflicted as our Friend, it would be that he should take the release given by the Church and say no more. Such a course seems to me more in proportion to the past, and more in harmony with what I could desire for the future. But this must be determined by intimate personal and private reasons, of which I am not in a position to judge ... But I can never clear my mind of the thought, that a wife may yet be saved by a husband (I mean for the world beyond the Grave – in this world all is dead and lost forever) and that his power of saving her will be according to his state and character of mind. A second marriage would be a final act, not of separation only but of *opposition*. A woman ceases to feel that she has wronged a man who is again happier than herself ... I do not see how Sin can make a woman cease to be always a wife. The prodigal was still a son, and would have been had he been lost eternally

... I say nothing of the effect of such an aim as prayers upon the husband: though I believe nothing would more deeply sanctify his own soul, or more powerfully intercede with God for the salvation of his unhappy life.

With these feelings you will easily see how the inclination I have to abide by the Law and interpretation of the Western Church becomes strong enough for a practical conclusion ... Ever yours affectionately, H.E. Manning.

Lincoln's convictions must have coincided with the views he expressed to Gladstone at the time of the Divorce Bill in 1857: 'I have no doubt of the Divine sanction of Divorce for cause of Adultery and feel convinced of its Social propriety – and though I do not think the Scriptural authority for re-marriage is *as* distinct, I believe it to be in accordance with the teaching of the Bible and with the objects of the Institution of Marriage. I do not remember any *direct* sanction of re-marriage after the *death* of a Wife or Husband and yet the permission to do so is never doubted.'[n]

Meanwhile, anxious to escape the scandal about to break, ill and distracted, he had been advised to go abroad and was preparing to leave on the yacht *Gitana* for a long journey to the Levant, embracing Constantinople and Egypt. Robert Renebald, his youngest brother, the Cherubim of other days, was to accompany him, but Lincoln found he could not shake off the binding spell. 'Poor unhappy Being!' he wrote[84] of Suzie to his old tutor. '*Her* sorrows are only now beginning, soon she will feel some portion of what she has made me suffer – and I can call God to witness that at this moment I feel no sentiment of bitterness towards *her,* but such mourning yearning compassion as the memory of the days when I hoped to find in her a Wife not only in name but in heart ...' But uppermost in his mind was the necessity for Susan's repentance. He wrote of this to Gladstone ('Received a letter from Lincoln that made me stagger with admiration'),[85] and on his last Sunday in England went down to Lavington in Sussex to see Manning, who, writing of this visit to Gladstone, described how 'his sorrow and his manliness go to my heart'. He had required to know of Manning whether 'the likelihood of repentance be less, after a prompt and complete severance [divorce], than it would be if the process were for a while hanging over her head, though with certainty at last'.[86] (This conversation was held on the day after Suzie was last seen vagabonding towards Mantua.) Mrs Gladstone, too, visualized a 'penitentiary, where for say a year she could be with a kind judicious friend and under *good discipline*! Archdeacon Manning at the head – might she not come out a new woman?'[87] Nor had Gladstone quite done. He held Lincoln in the greatest esteem: 'He has a very high creation, written by the hand of God, in the lineaments of his own character, its splendid integrity, its bravery, its manful will, and its deep affection', and while acknowledging 'how small one feels in recommending fine things on paper to the man who has to *do* them', after much heart-searching he was convinced that divorce was expedient. Yet 'the present Ecclesiastical Divorce *plus* the Act of Parliament do not make up a divorce *a circulo*,' he continued in his letter to Manning. 'The former does not profess it – the latter is powerless ... the only authority for divorce is the private persuasion acting upon a view of Scripture', and reaffirmed that Lincoln 'must not shrink from it, and he will not. If the steel could feel in the fire, it would writhe as he does.'[88] Having searched his conscience on religious grounds he now volunteered his assistance on the legal side, giving Mr Parkinson the benefit of evidence acquired at Naples and Como.

It was learned in October that Suzie was in Florence and that the Hamiltons and Lord Douglas were anxious that every facility should be given to effect a divorce and that Mr Ranken, their family solicitor, had undertaken to appear for Susan 'to any process that may be issued'. Prompted by this information, and by a loving heart, Mrs Gladstone again showed her affection and wrote to Suzie – '*you* whom I have once so tenderly loved', – but 'oh with what feelings: alas alas though too late to undo what has been done, dreadful as the sin is, thank God it is never too late to repent ... Oh by our early friendship let my words speak to you ... I cling to the hope they may not be written in vain. The door is yet open to you, a merciful God is ever ready to lead back the wandering sheep ... And now I would end my sad letter & still subscribe myself, if you will receive it, as Your friend Catherine Gladstone.'[89] The letter was conveyed through Gladstone and Parkinson to Ranken, who undertook to forward it to Susan. Three weeks later it was returned, and Gladstone wrote to Mr Parkinson.

                                        Fasque, Dec 1 1849[90]
Please to examine the enclosed as well as you can. It came to my

wife yesterday in this state except that I have cut open at the end the inner cover to avoid redisturbing the seal, & have taken out my wife's note which was in it just in the same state as when it went. You will observe Lady L received, read & resealed & returned it. Is this bravado? Do you know the handwriting of the outer cover?

Parkinson's reply is not without interest since it demonstrates once again Suzie's power of self-justification, her ability to lay the blame for almost everything (except pregnancy) elsewhere, and to exaggerate the dangers to her health.

> 66 Lincolns Inn Field[91]
> 3rd December 1849
>
> Mr Ranken ... called on me one day last week [Parkinson replied] with a letter from Lady Lincoln desiring him to return Mrs Gladstone's Letter, and stating that if she had known from whom it came she would not have opened it, but that she had not read it. He therefore came to me for your address and the enclosed Cover is in his handwriting. He read me, *in confidence,* Lady Lincoln's Letter, in which she is very severe upon you as having, as she states, been the cause of all her exposure, and is also severe upon Mrs Gladstone for writing to her. You were no doubt the occasion of ascertaining her state which was of course intended to have been kept secret ... She writes to Mr Ranken as if she was the injured person, and talks of speaking to Lord Brougham. In this Letter she also shews a very bad feeling towards Lord Lincoln. It seems that Lord Walpole was at the Villa near Como when you were there, and that when they first heard of you they thought it was Lord Lincoln, and Lord W crossed the lake between 2 and 3 in the morning, caught a violent cold, and was confined for some weeks. Lady L hurried to Verona and she was very seriously ill in her confinement and was not expected to live. My own impression is that Her Ladyship is deranged.

> Fasque Dec 6th 1849[92]
>
> I am sorry that Lady Lincoln feels resentment against the person who has been the cause of the exposure [Gladstone wrote] – quite irrespective of the question Whether that person happens to be myself ... My journey was merely the alternative, & the substitute for a severer measure. Had I not gone, a professional person

would have gone in my stead ... But I apprehend that especially as
the child lived it would have been impossible that he should fail to
discover it. If so, then not I, but the act has been the cause of the
exposure ... It was not I but a Higher Power that made me the
instrument of discovery.

It was perhaps the consequence of Catherine Gladstone's last letter
which led Suzie, some time later, to send Mrs Gladstone a message
through a common friend. 'Will you give her a message from me, a
terrible one? She is likely to see a great deal of my children. For most
things they could not be better than with her, but tell her that if she
ever speaks against their mother my ghost will haunt her. When she
is happy with her children let her think of me.' Mrs Gladstone, who
had frequently had the children to stay at Hawarden, and could perhaps gauge by that time the extent of their mother's affection, simply
exclaimed 'Oh, poor creature.'[93]

Suzie had reached Nice (then still in Italy) when she received Mrs
Gladstone's letter. Till then her time had been spent mostly in Florence, where meeting an acquaintance she 'carried it off with him as if
nothing had happened'. It is probable that she found a home there
for the baby, perhaps with nuns, or at a farm, for Walpole, having a
house in Florence, could provide the money for the child's keep. By
the time Suzie arrived in Nice on November 4th she had disposed of
it, and in February of the following year there was news for the Duke
of Newcastle from his solicitor.

Private

London Feb 23rd 1850[n]
My Lord Duke, Mr Parkinson called upon me today to mention
that the Child of which Lady Lincoln was delivered is dead. Mr
Parkinson thought your Grace should have the earliest intelligence
on the subject, but he at first doubted whether he should make
the communication until he had received some corroboration of
the report. The party however who gave him the information
stated that he might rely upon the fact and act accordingly, and
Mr Parkinson believes it to be true. The Child died abroad but he
did not know where. He did not mention the name of his infor-
mant.

Gladstone also received a communication from Parkinson: 'I have heard this afternoon and I believe from good authority, that Lady L's child, born at Verona, is dead.'[94] But at Nice in November 1849 these cares were not yet of a kind to trouble Suzie.

When Raphael, with Asman, had left Verona after Suzie's departure, he had gone to Como for a fortnight to collect further evidence, and had there engaged Trincavelli as his valet. From Milan Raphael went on to Florence where by chance he again found Susan at the same hotel as himself, calling herself by her correct name. Santi on recognizing him appeared exceedingly confused 'and even staggered against the wall'. From Florence Raphael returned to England with the result of his enquiries, leaving Asman, with Trincavelli as companion and interpreter, to await further instructions. Travelling first to Genoa and then to Nice, they put up at the Hotel des Etrangers on the rue du Pont Neuf in the old part of the town, much frequented by travellers, arriving there the day before Suzie. This was purely fortuitous, Asman having gone to Nice to idle away the time until he heard from Raphael. To his astonishment while sitting at his window he saw Susan, Job, and Santi drive up in the familiar travelling carriage. A few days later as he and Trincavelli were walking 'by the Sea Side' they were overtaken by an open carriage in which were seated Suzie and a 'tall elderly gentleman'. They were 'laughing and talking and her Ladyship, as I at first thought, was too occupied in her conversation to notice me, and they were driving very fast'. But after going a little way the coachman turned his horses and they drove slowly back, Susan having changed sides 'so as to be opposite me, and she looked hard at me as she passed and then I thought she recognized me, but I had allowed my mustachios to grow while I was abroad and this had altered my appearance'. He asked Trincavelli if he knew her. 'Yes, she is Madame Laurence the sister of Lord Walpole, my master at Como. Oh no, he [Asman] said, it is no Madame Laurence, it is Lady Lincoln. I told him I never knew her by that name. He told me I knew nothing at all about it.' The next Sunday Asman saw her again at the English Church. He had taken his seat when she came in and was about to sit on the same side as himself, when she recognized him, looked confused, and moved to the other side. After the service she walked away with the same elderly man; this might possibly have been Sir Charles Lamb, Bt, aged sixty-four, eighteen months a widower, of whom the next year when writing to her mother, Charlotte Canning exclaimed: 'Surely the report of Ly Lincoln marrying Sir Charles Lamb cannot be true.'[95]

At the hotel Asman took his meals at the table d'hôte, while Trincavelli dined with the servants and was often at the same table as Job and Santi, who asked him 'what did the folks say about our going off so quick from Como. and I told him they said they did not know what to think, but that I had said as they bid me, that it was the Lady's Mother that was took ill'. Both Santi and Job were very silent after that. A few days later Asman learned of Lord Walpole's arrival at the Victoria Hotel in Nice, and that evening Trincavelli pointed him out walking by himself while the band was playing. Since leaving Varenna towards the end of August he had been seen at Cologne and was known to have 'written to his Bankers in England for money and a letter of credit to all parts of the Continent, as if he contemplated continuing his travels abroad'.[n] In September he had been at Ems for his health where he was seen by the Douglases, but though he sent a message to Lord Douglas that he was anxious to speak to him, only a word or two was exchanged and that out of doors.[96]

On November 16th Asman received a letter from Raphael containing a citation for divorce and instructions to serve it on Suzie, and then to come home. Asman wrote a respectful letter saying he had some papers to show her and requesting an interview to which she agreed. He found Santi in the room with her and delivered to her the sealed document.

The Duke of Newcastle's health was deteriorating seriously. Early in 1850 he left Clumber with his daughters for the Victoria Hotel, St Leonards-on-Sea, occupying apartments recently vacated by Louis Philippe and his family. His correspondence with Suzie's father had not altogether ceased, and his estrangement from his son enabled him perhaps to overlook the way in which the Duke managed to convey, though handling it with remarkable delicacy, that the 'melancholy event that is now, as you justly observe, clothing us all in sack cloth and ashes, in sorrow and shame' was as much the fault of Lincoln as of his own daughter. Perhaps it managed to assuage the Duke of Hamilton's pride which had been deeply shocked. 'This melancholy affair in which we are all involved, is advancing & – I grieve to say – is gradually making its way into the mouths of the Publick. We are miserable. The Duchess in despair & you will sympathize with us as we sympathize with you, in the common calamity of the whole family – for you like myself come within the sphere of this distressing scene.'[n] There were reports of common ill health they could also share. The Duke of Hamilton had been almost 'carried out of this world altogether, by an obstinate catarrh that lasted six weeks nearly, & has left me in such a state of *delicate* sensibility, that I am obliged to get into the fire, & live like a salamander in the flames, to avoid being turned into, not a pillar of salt, but of fire'.[n] Had the Duke of Newcastle not been totally without guile one might have suspected him of malice as he sent the following message to Scotland. 'You know, I presume, what is said to be going on. I have been told that Lady Walpole means to divorce her Husband, for which she possesses sufficient evidence – & lately I am assured that the child is dead. If Ly W succeeds in divorcing her husband, in all probability the sequel will be an union of the criminals, which I lament & readily suppose will be by no means agreeable to you.'[h] By the spring the Duke was in sufficient health to come to London and, still with his daughters, visited the zoological gardens to see the hippopotamus just arrived, an expedition which in its dénouement held the rudiments of minor tragedy. 'One of my daughters came up & told me that we had just passed two of Lincoln's children,' he wrote in his diary, 'Edward, the second boy, & the daughter Susan. She said they were close by & that the boy in the blue jacket was Edward. I looked at him with wonder for I could not recognize a feature of his countenance or see any likeness to his family. The girl, I afterwards found, I had even touched as I passed her on the walk & heard her voice but did not know her though she is less altered than the boy. I subsequently came up to them near where the hippopotamus is kept & renewed my acquaintance with them. They were very civil & well behaved as two strangers, & stared at me very much, but showed no emotion. They came with Mrs Gladstone.'

Divorce proceedings moved slowly. There were a great many witnesses to examine, some of them Italian, who plagued Mr Parkinson considerably, but by May 2nd the case was complete and would be heard on the 13th. From the opposite side the suit had been facilitated which Gladstone hoped 'may be a sign of penitence or may not'. No provision for such a likelihood as divorce having been made, the Duke of Hamilton suggested that Suzie should forfeit her jointure from the Newcastle estates, but receive the income from her own property. The Duke of Newcastle felt reassured by his solicitor who reminded him that 'a year had elapsed with the channel between them – one of the parties had been "extra quattuor maria", as in olden times they used to say, at the time the child was begotten. In the present instance the absence of the parties from each other exceeds a year.'[h]

The Bill was heard in the House of Lords for the first time on May 13th, when a copy of the proceedings in the Consistory Court of London was presented at the Bar of the House. On the 28th the witnesses were called, including Mr Gladstone, and on that day the Duke of Newcastle wrote in his diary that Lincoln's divorce Bill 'has passed the 2nd reading. His vile & abandoned Wife offered no defence.' Lord Brougham, who had known the Duke of Hamilton since his days at Edinburgh in 1800, had charge of the Bill and had done all he could to forward it through the House. There was a rumour about that he had received Suzie and Walpole at Cannes when he knew them to be having 'criminal connexion with each other'. This he vehemently denied as a 'most absurd tissue of mis-statements'; neither had been under his roof for a single day since he had heard that a suit had been instituted in the ecclesiastical courts. (Early in 1851, in referring to a recent period, he told the Duke of Hamilton that 'nothing could be more amiable & delicate than Ly S[usan]'s proceedings with respect to me. She had intended to come to Cannes to pass a week – but as she was not alone, she passed on considering that it would have been unpleasant to me to say I could *only receive herself* – because from what passed last year she knew that must be.'[h]) Neither Suzie nor Walpole had been to England for two years, and at the time of the divorce were said to be living 'in open adultery' in Rome. Brougham had cautioned them not to winter in Pisa, being 'but an hour's drive from Florence', presumably because Lady Walpole lived there. At the very end of May, after an Amendment was read and agreed to by the House, the Bill to dissolve Lincoln's marriage and enable him to remarry was passed.

After ten months abroad Lincoln was now on his way home. The Bosphorus, the interest of Ephesus, Patmos and Rhodes, Easter at Jerusalem, Tyre, Sidon, Baalbek, all these had refreshed him and his health had improved, though an unexpected reminder of Walpole which he encountered in Egypt was of almost crippling intensity. Upon entering the temple at El Kab 'almost before I looked at any of the sculpture or hieroglyphics, my eye caught on the wall (though written in small letters) the name of W 1837! I cannot say how indescribable the effect upon me was – it turned me sick & I sat down on a broken fragment of a column for some minutes. That Name! – & alas to me that year* also.'[n] In mid July a rough sea brought him to Gibraltar in nine days from Malta. He was now eager for England ('I grow so impatient to see my Children again that I can apply myself to nothing') but news of the death of Sir Robert Peel, to Lincoln a very severe blow, darkened his return. To Gladstone he wrote: 'I really can hardly picture to myself any event except the loss of one of my Children which would bring such poignant sorrow to my blighted heart', for 'the sorrows of my domestic life have been so associated with his ready and friendly Counsels, and I have ever found in him so delicate a sympathy and so sagacious advice, that the termination of my married life and the simultaneous death of Friend and Counsellor seem to leave me in a void which yet appears bewildering.'[n]

By the late autumn of 1850 the Duke of Newcastle was extremely ill. From Clumber Lincoln was obliged to write to the Duke of Hamilton explaining how 'this morning my poor Father called for pen and paper, having been unable to write or read for the last three months. Having, as I suppose he imagined, finished the letter, he sent for my Brother Robert & told him to date it "Clumber" & sign it "Newcastle". He did so, & thus was enabled to see that not only was it not legible but there was not a word or letter formed. Some three or four hours afterwards he again sent for Robert, told him to seal it and direct it to you. Robert tells me you cannot possibly believe it to be anything but the scribble of a Child.' His mind was not entirely affected, for in some respects his memory was sound and his intellect quite clear, but he was subject to fits of violent passion, and though the lower part of his body and bowels were paralyzed, Lincoln could speak of '*no* actual or tangible malady'.[h] Another obsession was his utter disregard of money. 'You know not the misery I have to undergo here,' Lincoln wrote to a friend. 'My father has no other care or thought than to order every sort of extravagance both in the shape of purchases & works, & to raise money to pay for them in every possible & impossible objectionable way, & this with his

---

* The year of Suzie's terrible illness in Paris, the cause of which had been her love affair with Lincoln's brother.

affairs on the verge of bankruptcy!' The Duke's 'unamiable and unnatural sentiments' were such that Lincoln was 'obliged to forego the society of my little girl & youngest boy all the time I have been here, & even now that my others are coming home (alas I should not have written that word for they have *none*) for their holidays he will not have any of them in the house. I am obliged therefore to find *some* doss to shelter them.'[n] Towards Christmas he stayed at Windsor Castle for three nights, the Queen writing in her Journal on December 22nd that 'Ld Lincoln sat again next to me at dinner. I pity him so much for besides his conjugal misfortunes, his father has entirely ruined the property, continuing to do so, & he has the prospect of being left penniless.'[97]

Lord William had died in September soon after his brother's divorce, but the Duke had not been told. Now as the winter silence fell on the park and upon the house where his father lay dying, Lincoln would have remembered that time just fourteen years ago, when the discovery of William's letter to his wife had been the beginning of so much pain. By his father's death in January 1851, Lincoln inherited enormous debts, and the ruin of a fortune; he also assumed the honours, state, dignities of the 5th Duke of Newcastle.

Abroad, Suzie too was undergoing a change of name. Her father and Lord Brougham had both advised it,[h] and though unwilling, as being 'une chose inusitée [unusual]', and reluctant to have to give explanations to acquaintances, she nevertheless agreed to call herself by the earlier appellation of Lady Susan Hamilton, not without lamenting that she had 'alas, struggled through too many sore trials during my unhappy existence with L' to care to retain his name after such cruel sufferings.[h] But there was to be a final transition in 1862, when at the British Consulate, Naples, to the dismay of her family, she married a tradesman's son, Jean Alexis Opdebeeck, her Belgian courier.

10

The Farce Played Out

The Duke of Hamilton did not long survive. At his death in the summer of 1852, Charlotte Canning picked up the information that he had 'left Lady Lincoln an annuity of 700 a year only'.[98] It was in fact £250 every six months until the death of the Duchess, which occurred in 1859, when she would inherit the 'Salisbury [Beckford] property' for life. The Duchess had left her a small annuity, an ivory casket with all its contents, her music bound and unbound, shawls and laces. But Suzie, living a nomadic life abroad, had not troubled to come to England to see her 'ever lamented Mamina' in her last illness, but wrote to her brother about the dispersal of her mother's furs, even enquiring of the French maid 'What has been done about the furs?'[99] Lord Douglas, now the 11th Duke, had been generous to her, but after Suzie's second marriage broke off all communication, dreading her influence on his children, who, according to an observer in about 1860, were deplorably brought up by their German-born mother, who preferred to live abroad as 'a foreign princess rather than an English duchess'.[100] After Douglas's death in Paris in 1863 she refused to see Suzie and was much vexed on learning that at Vichy Susan had desired to meet Napoleon III (whom Marie claimed as a cousin), for the Emperor was receiving hourly despatches in connection with her brother's illness and death. To Suzie it was a 'dreadful dream to think that our loved Douglas is no more. God grant indeed that the fatal bereavement may be sanctified to us all.' It appeared to her 'but a short time since the one I now mourn stood before me in all his glorious beauty'. Of her sister-in-law, she had 'long appreciated her as she deserves. I see the injured sister is the one who forgot unkindness whilst the wife who *caused* the estrangement remembers! I can never doubt *his* heart & I know what it was till it fell into her keeping.' Even Madge's long-standing devotion to her cousin was sorely tried, and she admitted that to her Suzie was 'a complete enigma. Her letters are curiosities, for really she says such marvells to different people.'[101]

Susan came rarely to England. Gladstone, at St Andrew's, Wells Street, on Easter Day, 1854, thought he 'saw poor Lady L from afar'.[102] Occasionally, abroad, she saw her children as they grew up. But except for Edward, the second son, who laudably fulfilled his heritage, the children were no credit to their father, who for twelve years struggled alone, as his own father had done before him, to bring them up to his high and inflexible standards. Misfortune had dogged his life, and his last years were overshadowed with grief. Manning, whom he had loved as a friend and spiritual counsellor, had been received into the Roman Church in 1851, a step which filled the Duke with 'grief such as no similar event has ever occasioned to me before'.[h] Earlier, anticipating the irrevocable step, he had written to Manning:[103]

I have not heard from you since ... I parted from you at Lavington, broken in heart and health, but with a lively and consoling recollection of you – your parish – your Church – your peaceful graveyard* – your Communion-table, which often recurred to me in lands far distant and in perils by sea. Your affectionate kindness is so entwined with the deepest affliction of an unhappy life as almost to appear a mitigation of its intensity. You stand to me in the double relationship of a dear private friend and one to whom I have long been accustomed to look up as a Guide and Instructor in matters of Religion and Faith ... You love the Church ... you love her still ... Surely in this her hour of trial it were cowardice to leave her ramparts† – but it were treason to go over to the Assailants ... We ought to strive more than ever to repair the breach ... and not desert through the gate before which is arrayed the army of Rome.

On the day it was received, Manning replied:[n]

Among many letters which this time has brought me, none has

* Where Manning's wife lay buried beside her sister, Samuel Wilberforce's wife. Here Wilberforce himself would lie in 1873.
† Probably a reference to the Church of Rome claiming many converts. Cardinal Wiseman had been installed as Archbishop of Westminster; protests against 'Papal agression' were to follow.

moved me more than yours. All our past thoughts of sorrow gave
to its affectionate forbearance a force beyond words ... In truth
my heart is almost broken. All human love, all that makes life precious to me, except one thing, is passing or past away ... When the
thought, even the sight of my home [paper torn] and Church come
over me my heart breaks and no human solace so much as touches
me. The only thing left is a conscience clear & at peace ... And yet
if human love, or sorrow or any lower motive had held me when
truth & conscience bade me decide, I should have been more
unworthy still ...

In 1852 the Duke had been appointed Secretary of State for the
Colonies, a position he held for two years, when on the outbreak of
the Crimean War, and until the government resigned early in 1855,
he carried, as Secretary for War, the responsibility for its conduct.
His health suffered under the shattering strain, and when his nine-
year-old son, Lord Albert, offered him a medical prescription, his
father could only reply that 'nothing but the taking of Sebastopol can
do me any good at present'.

By now the Duke's devotion to the beautiful Lady Waldegrave was
generally known. He made her his confidante, enlisting her help with
his daughter whom by 1857 he was launching into Society. Lady
Waldegrave, who had had a varied career, was married to an elderly
husband, but she took delight in championing her friends, had a certain political influence, and listened sympathetically as the Duke
poured out to her his troubles. By 1859 (and again Secretary for the
Colonies) his source of deepest sorrow was his daughter Susan, over
whom he had watched with anxious care for fear she might tread the
same path as her mother. Writing to his old friend Charlotte Canning, far off in India, he told her his daughter was as much admired
for her behaviour and manners as for her beauty, and that in Society
she was called '"Semiramide", and she certainly has a very Queen-
like look'. For two years her hand had been sought by Lord Adolphus Vane-Tempest (Dolly), favourite son of the redoubtable Frances
Anne, second wife of the Marquess of Londonderry, herself a
'dumpy, rum-shaped and rum-faced article',[104] according to Creevey
the diarist. He was in every way an unsuitable match: he had gam-
bled away his money, he was subject to attacks of near-insanity
(probably tertiary syphilis) when four keepers were required to hold

him down, and he was fourteen years her senior.* The Duke categorically refused his consent and forbade any correspondence. Susan was determined to marry him. In London a few days before she came of age, as the Duke was stepping into his brougham on his way to Clumber, a letter was put in his hand. Dolly renewed his marriage proposal and requested an interview of the Duke; both were summarily refused. Lady Londonderry was only concerned for the happiness of her son, though later she bitterly repented having favoured the match.

A few weeks later Susan, accompanied by her governess (who was obliged to ask a woman in the street to lend them money and call a cab – the Duke having forbidden his servants to fetch one, and refusing his own carriage), drove from Portman Square to St Mary's, Bryanston Square, empty but for a witness on the bridegroom's side and Susan's eldest brother who gave her in marriage. Dolly trembled so during the ceremony that they expected a fit.[105] Only two years previously Susan had been bridesmaid to the Princess Royal, and Queen Victoria writing to her daughter was shocked to think that 'one of your bridesmaids & really a clever, agreeable, handsome girl should do such a thing'.[106] Only think,' the Queen had written, 'Lady Susan P. Clinton has gone and married Ld Adolphus Vane, who drinks and has twice been shut up for delirium tremens … Lord Adolphus is a good creature and not the one who did all those dreadful things, but between drink and his natural tendency to madness there is a sad prospect for poor Susan.'[107] (It had been his brother, Lord Ernest, who had earned the reputation for doing 'dreadful things' by his propensity for attacking actresses at Windsor.) Ten days later, on May 5th, the Queen had further information: 'Think how horrid – they say that Lord Adolphus Vane is already gone mad and shut up',[108] for before the honeymoon was over he had thrown forks, knives and a decanter at his wife.

Dolly had a severe attack at the end of 1860 and was packed off to a home in Queen Street, Edinburgh, but had sufficiently recovered to go to France in February for Lord Lincoln's wedding. Susan had been on bad terms with Lady Londonderry for months, principally because of her extravagances and debts, for which her mother-in-

---

* His sister, married to the sixth Duke of Marlborough, was the mother of Lord Randolph Churchill.

law, vigorously resenting such conduct, was applied to for payment. 'I have been very angry with Susan', she wrote to her son, 'but have no explanation or excuse beyond that "she will pay them", which knowing she can have no money is both false and absurd. I am utterly out of all patience with Susan, with her 28 boxes & her endless extravagance & I see nothing but misery & perdition in store for you both.' Susan's father had given her no trousseau and had made her no settlement, and Lady Londonderry thought that 'No allowance could ever cover these lists of debts & it is ridiculous to talk of one, or of giving money to a girl who really seems not to know a shilling from a pound.' On another occasion she reminded Dolly that 'When you talk of the position you have taken her from, I must observe that she has been careful not to deny herself any thing. I *know* she has stated she could have married Ld Cowper. Ld Ward & I equally *know* this to be untrue.'* From France Susan wrote her a letter for her birthday to which she replied with 'many thanks for your tardy civility', though in private commenting at its being a 'Very toadying epistle *I* think'.[109]

At the beginning of 1861 the Duke's eldest son Henry, now Lord Lincoln, or Linky, contracted a marriage in Paris with Henrietta, daughter of the millionaire Henry Hope. She had been born out of wedlock (though Hope had later married the girl's mother), and the Duke refused to countenance the marriage. Linky, 'very worthless I fear', according to Queen Victoria,[110] was notorious for his huge racing debts, so that when Lady Londonderry wrote of Lord Lincoln's marriage having been 'talked of in England & not pleasantly, as it is known that illegitimacy & gambling debts made the *fond* for the barter of Wealth & Rank, & it is thought the young Lady has been sold for a ducal coronet', she was probably telling no more than the truth. 'He, who was obliged to fly the country', she continued to Lord Adolphus, '& could not shew his face but for his marriage, & has not one 6d but Mr Hope's money – fortunate indeed that he did marry, or where wd you be having backed his bills for thousands?'[111] Hope paid Linky's debts on the understanding that after the marriage

---

* George, 7th Earl Cowper, was immensely rich. He had succeeded in 1856 at the age of twenty-two; at the death of his mother he inherited the Barony of Lucas. He married the daughter of the Marquess of Northampton. Lord Ward's reputation was notoriously shocking.

the couple would reside with him at Deepdene, Surrey, or at his
house in Piccadilly. A tight financial rein was kept on Linky, so that
having abetted his sister's marriage with a wastrel, and thinking to
profit from the arrangement (Dolly having gone surety for large
sums), he now found himself unable to guarantee a loan to Lord
Adolphus.

On the night of Linky's wedding, February 11th, 1861, Mrs Hope
had given a large dinner following the wedding breakfast, at which a
good deal of wine was drunk, and Dolly had 'added considerably to
his potations'; while abroad, though owning to a régime of 'half a
bottle of light claret in water at luncheon, and ½ at dinner', he had
not admitted to 'brandy and liqueurs on the sly'. Susan, alarmed by
his 'admonitory symptoms', had a fit of hysterics and returned to her
hotel with her husband, followed shortly by her uncle, Lord Charles
Pelham-Clinton, and by her mother (Suzie) who was living in Paris,
and was thought to be 'the cause of much mischief to their marriage',
for Susan had been seen 'driving all over Paris' with her mother and
'going to Plays &c'. Lord Charles lived in Brussels with his wife and
children – eventually there were seven – and admitted to having
'barely enough to keep body & soul together'. This particular
evening Dolly, having promised to go to bed (it was believed he had
done so), went out 'to a House the nature of which you will understand', Charles informed Dolly's elder brother, Lord Vane, '& ended
by going to the Café Anglais where he insulted, & hit (being mad
drunk) a French & American Gentleman', who fortunately behaved
well and gave him into the custody of the police, from which Suzie
and Mr Hope eventually recovered him. The following night much
the same occurred, and on the third evening three men were required
to manage him when he became violent; even so he contrived to
break his bed. Half way through this long descriptive letter, Lord
Charles was taken ill with 'spasms in the throat', but concluded by
recalling that 'of all the places in the world for a man with such
propensities, Paris is the worst; there are such facilities for every kind
of excess'.[112]

Once back in London, Lord Adolphus told his brother that he was
taking rooms at Stevens's Hotel [New Bond Street], and on being re-
monstrated with that 'Stevens's is not a place for a lady to go to, its
being a man's Hotel', Dolly replied: 'Lady Susan will go to the Hotel
her husband thinks best.' However, when a further fearful outbreak

followed, Susan had a miscarriage (putting an end to the 'dreadful bon-mot' about herself and Dolly which the Queen passed on to her daughter: 'There is a bet which of the two will be confined first!!'),[113] and Dolly was taken to a house at St John's Wood, with attendant doctors and four men,[114] while Susan, unwilling to be with her own mother, was obliged to go to her husband's. 'I know it will be painful to you,' wrote Lord Vane to Lady Londonderry, who was reported to have said she would 'sooner by half that she [Susan] threw a glass of water in my face than put on that detestable passive look', but she 'is generally under the influence of opium & hardly knows what she does or says'.[115]

On the recommendation of his doctors Dolly sailed to America in the summer for four months, in search of health. Home again, and after further attacks, he was 'quite maniacal' and behaving 'like a wild animal' in the early part of 1864. By June he was dead. 'I forgot to tell you', wrote the Queen to her daughter from Windsor Castle, on Waterloo Day, 'that poor Susan Vane's dreadful husband died ... – I believe in a struggle with four keepers when he burst a vein in his throat. She is left penniless ... He tried to kill her last week and also the child – so that I believe it is to her a real release too.'[116] Susan survived her husband for a little over ten years, but her brother Arthur predeceased her. He too had proved a spendthrift and wholly irresponsible, being liable in 1861 for nearly £15,000 worth of debts and having 'beyond all doubt, been very, very, foolish', according to one of his friends. Added to which he appeared enslaved by an unmentionable perversion of which there was a foretaste in a letter from Linky to Dolly, referring to Arty at Versailles, at the age of twenty-one, writing on *mauve scented paper with his initials in red & a coronet in gold'*, and 'running up a bill of 130 frs to a coiffeur!!!'[117] He died from scarlet fever at Christchurch in 1870 while on bail, charged in a murky case of 'Men in Women's Attire', heard at the Central Criminal Court. Shortly afterwards, Albert, the baby for whom the Prince Consort had stood godfather, married a woman who shut herself up in a Roman Catholic convent in Kensington, only to escape from it at night two weeks later and move in with the co-respondent in the divorce which followed. When in his turn Linky died at a London hotel in 1879, his mother at Nice, having survived the death of three sons and a daughter, found herself 'crushed and broken, body & mind', unable to believe that 'the comfort and joy of my life has gone'.[118] Of the Duke's five children, one only, Edward, seems to have escaped some portion of the aberrations traced back, through their mother, to William Beckford, nor was he apparently affected by the upbringing, rigid and oppressive, of an intolerant father.

But Suzie's sixth child ('my pickle', as she referred to him), Horatio Walpole – falsely reported to have died in infancy, probably reared by nuns in Italy, educated at Heidelberg University, made a ward of Chancery to avoid possession by an itinerant mother – lived and prospered. His father, succeeding as Earl of Orford in 1858 and now a noted misogynist, lived on until 1894, every link with Suzie severed soon after her divorce.

At the beginning of 1864 the Duke of Newcastle's health was starting to fail. He resigned his office, and died at Clumber in October. The widowed Queen Victoria had been to take farewell of him in June; immediately she had heard his life was in danger she had come up from Windsor to London, and accompanied by Arthur Stanley, Dean of Westminster, had gone to 'where the poor Duke was lying in his bed. Though looking drawn & pinched, the countenance was unaltered & he gave me a look of the kindest recognition which I shall not forget! I took hold of his hand saying "God bless you" & told him what a kind friend he had been to us both.'[119] He must also have found consolation – if anything could comfort him – in a letter from Cardinal Manning,[n] who hearing of his illness, wrote in sympathy from Rome, strengthening him in the courage he had never lacked, thinking it 'a great thing to wear out, & I never can think any man to have cause for regret, in this sense, who wears out early & in full work'.

> It seems to me but the other day [he continued] when we were all starting from Oxford into active life, little knowing what a future was before us, & how our paths would part asunder. I have always looked upon yours as one of the most useful and consistent public lives of those who begun so full of hope thirty years ago.

Although, in a different sense, Suzie's life had also been passed much in the public eye, since her divorce it had moved progressively into shadow. Without much beyond her own health and circumstance to occupy her thoughts, her figure had become heavy, she was always in financial straits, and friends had fallen away. She moved between France and Italy, seeking a mild climate and therapeutic waters, but in 1860 she settled in Paris, to her brother's disgust, for he too had a house there, in which he died. A great bond of sympathy with her ill-starred son-in-law Dolly compelled her to write to him from La Spezia in 1861 (when she was recovering from bronchitis followed by scarlet fever), wishing she had heard in time of his going to America, for she would have offered herself as a companion. Later, she could not rejoice at her daughter's pregnancy, '& I tremble for the future but she was wild for having a child & seemed to forget the malady it might inherit!'[120]

Although she had previously gone through some kind of ceremony in Paris with her courier, most probably in early 1860, it was not until December 1862 that they were legally married in Naples, Jean Alexis Opdebeeck giving his age as forty years, Suzie reducing hers by five; she was then forty-eight. That summer she had written to her cousin to acquaint her of an event deeply involving her happiness, 'I mean my marriage with Mr Opdebeeck a Belgian. We were privately married at Paris but did not declare it for several reasons. Now finding that the report has reached England, not wishing to give rise to false & ill-natured interpretations, we have decided to admit the fact, & we are having it legalized according to Belgian laws.' Their first marriage had taken place while she was seriously ill, her *'friend'* wishing to have the right to nurse her, 'and willingly did I give the right to one who had comforted me in sorrow & nursed me in suffering. I felt I was perfectly independent & should be foolish to sacrifice my happiness to *worldly* consideration, & for the sake of those who did nothing for me.'[121]

Opdebeeck's father, from near Malines, seems to have been a farmer, though Suzie's marriage certificate describes him as 'Merchant';* his mother was the daughter of a brewer whose grandfather was illiterate. How long they remained together is not known, though he was with her when she died; Suzie was in England in the 1880s, near Croydon first, moving on to Bournemouth, and finally to some rooms in a home at Keymer, near Burgess Hill in Sussex. He was alive when she made her will in 1881, leaving him 'All property of whatsoever kind over which I shall have power thus to dispose',

---

* Probably a rough translation of the French 'marchand' (tradesman).

which at her death eight years later amounted to £300 which passed
to a creditor in Germany. Besides her personal estate she would still
have derived income from Beckford property which perhaps enabled
her to live in some comfort at Wynnstay, the large red brick Victo-
rian house at Keymer where she had rooms, and where she died in
1889 on November 28th, the day after the anniversary of her marriage to Lincoln. Perhaps one or other of her two surviving sons
raised the stone which marks her grave in St John's cemetery, Burgess
Hill: Lord Edward Pelham-Clinton, then groom-in-waiting to Queen
Victoria, but once the baby weaned at Clumber to facilitate the bud-
ding love affair between mother and uncle – the turning point in
Suzie's tempestuous life; or Horatio Walpole, the offspring of its
zenith. The carved ivy branch, symbol of clinging memory, gracefully
entwining the gravestone under which she lies, may perhaps ensure a
lingering thought for giddy, light-hearted, faithless Suzie, if only for
the manner in which she touched Mr Gladstone's life during that
oppressively hot Italian summer, when he struggled so conscientiously to rescue her as she scampered down the primrose path.

Reference Notes

Index

Reference Notes

LIST OF ABBREVIATIONS

Chapeau Coil. The Abbé Chapeau, Private Collection
Gladstone Diaries *The Gladstone Diaries,* ed M. R. D. Foot and H. C. G. Matthew, 1974, iv
Gladstone Papers Gladstone Papers, British Museum
Hagley Papers In the possession of Viscount Cobham
St Deiniol's St Deiniol's Library, Hawarden (Newcastle MSS)

SOURCE REFERENCES

h Hamilton Papers, Lennoxlove, East Lothian
n Newcastle Papers, University of Nottingham Library

1. *Days of the Dandies,* Lord Lamington, *Blackwood Magazine,* 1890
2. *Diaries and Correspondence of the First Earl of Malmesbury,* ed by the Third Earl, 1844, iv, 392
3. *La Paolina,* F de l'Angle, 1946, 269
4. *Pauline,* W. N. Carlton, 1931, 354
5. *Letters* of *Harriet, Countess Granville,* ed F. Leveson-Gower, 1894, i, 269–70
6. *Ibid.,* 355
7. *Life at Fonthill,* ed Boyd Alexander, 1957, 284
8–10. Harrowby MSS Trust
11. *Letters of Harriet, Countess Granville,* ii, 210
12. Gladstone Papers
13. 14. *Gazette des Tribuneaux,* Édition de Paris, 9 décembre, 1837
15. *The Beast and the Monk,* S. Chitty, 1974, 83
16. *Gaglignani's Messenger,* December 14, 1837
17. *Gazette des Tribuneaux,* 9 décembre, 1837
18. St Deiniol's
19. *Private Letters of Sir Robert Peel,* ed George Peel, 5920, 593, 195
20–28. St Deiniol's
29. *Gladstone Diaries,* iii, 295
30–34. St Deiniol's
35. *Scenes and Memories,* Walburga Lady Paget, 1913, 172
36. St Deiniol's. Copy in Mr Gladstone's hand of Extract from Lady Walpole's affidavit, which he carried with him to Como.
37. *Spas of Germany,* A. B. Granville, 1843, 544
38. Lady Canning's Papers, Leeds
39. St Deiniol's
40–41. Gladstone Papers
42–45. St Deiniol's
46–48. Gladstone Papers
49. St Deiniol's
50. Gladstone Papers
51. Chapeau Coil.
52. Hagley Papers
53. *Gladstone Diaries,* 131

54. *Ibid.,* 133
55. Gladstone Papers
56. *The Parting of Friends,* D. Newsome, 1966, 322
57, 58. Chapeau Coll.
59. *Gladstone Diaries,* 136
60. Gladstone Papers
61–69. St Deiniol's
70. Hagley Papers
71. *Gladstone Diaries,* 143
72–76. St Deiniol's
77. *Gladstone Diaries,* 143
78. *Ibid.,* 144
79. Gladstone Papers
80. *Gladstone Diaries,* 148
81. *Life of Gladstone,* J. Morley, 1903, i, 365
82. Gladstone Papers
83. Chapeau Coll.
84. St Deiniol's
85. *Gladstone Diaries,* 155
86. Chapeau Coll.
87. *Mrs Gladstone,* G. Battiscombe, 1956, 75
88. Gladstone Papers
89. St Deiniol's
90. Gladstone Papers
91. St Deiniol's
92. Gladstone Papers
93. *Mrs Gladstone,* 76
94. St Deiniol's
95. Lady Canning's Papers
96. St Deiniol's
97. Queen Victoria's Journals
98. Lady Canning's Papers
99. Harrowby MSS Trust
100. *The Linings of Life,* Walburga Lady Paget, 1928, i, 63
101. Harrowby MSS Trust
102. *Gladstone Diaries,* 611
103. Chapeau Coll.
104. *Frances Anne,* Edith, Marchioness of Londonderry, 1958, 135
105. *My Dear Duchess,* ed A. L. Kennedy, 1956, 101–2
106. *Dearest Child,* ed R. Fulford. 1964. 250
107. *Ibid.,* 249
108. *Ibid.,* 252
109. *Ibid.,* 249
110–112. Londonderry Papers
113. *Dearest Child,* 251
114. Londonderry Papers
115. *My Dear Duchess,* 153–4
116. *Dearest Mama,* ed R. Fulford, 1968, 347–8
117. Londonderry Papers
118. Harrowby MSS Trust
119. Queen Victoria's Journals
120, 121. Harrowby MSS Trust

Index

Abercorn, 2nd Marquess of, 14
Aboyne, 4th Earl of, 6
Adam, Robert, 2
Adelaide, Queen, 25
Albert, Prince, 61, 65, 69, 131, 132
Allies, Rev. W. T., 93
Anglesea Ville, 56, 57, 59, 60, 63, 64, 65
Ashton Hall, 18, 27
Asman, Joseph, goes abroad, 110–11; recognizes S, 111; tricked by S, 112; at Nice, and recognized by S., 119; serves citation, 120
Augusta, Princess, 48

Bad Ems, 71, 72, 74, 75, 76, 79, 82, 89, 110, 120
Baden, 29, 73, 76, 81
Baden, Marie, Princess of, see Douglas and Clydesdale, Marchioness of
Baden, Stephanie, Grand Duchess of, 59, 73
Bagot, Emily, see Winchilsea, Countess of
Balzarri, Dottore, 103, 107
Bath, 16, 46, 66, 69
Bath, 2nd Marquess of, 39
Bathurst, Henry, Bishop of Norwich, 39
Beckford, Susan Euphemia, see Hamilton, Duchess of
Beckford, William, 17, 132; as father, 6; as collector, 7; French appellation, 46; death, 66
Bentinck, Lord George, 89
Bergamo, 107, 110

Berryer, maître, 46
Borghese, Princess Pauline, 5, 6
Brodick Castle, Isle of Arran, 5, 20, 80, 82
Brougham, Lord, 117, 122, 124
Brown, Mr, 18, 23
Brunswick, Duke of, 25
Butler, Samuel, Bishop of Lichfield, 39

Cambridge, Princess Augusta of, 64
Canning, Hon. Charles (later Viscount), 4, 15, 35, 47, 48
Canning, Viscountess, 35, 47, 48, 72, 120, 125, 127
Canino, Prince, 85
Carlile, Richard, 66
Carlton Club, 30
Charles X, King of France, 7
Châtelherault, duc de, see Hamilton, Duke of
Churchill, Lord Randolph, 128n
Clinton, Hon. Albert Pelham- (later Lord Albert), 124, 127; birth, 68, 74; worthless, 126; married and divorced, 131
Clinton, Hon. Arthur Pelham- (later Lord Arthur), 56, 72, 111, 126; birth, 48; illness, 66; worthless, 126, 131; charge of transvestism and death, 131
Clinton, Hon. Edward Pelham- (later Lord Edward), 34, 38, 40, 44, 45, 54, 57, 70; birth, 32; weaned, 36, 134; to Dover, 65; at zoo, 121; creditable, 126, 134

Clinton, Hon. Henry Pelham-
('Linky', later 13th Earl of Lincoln), 26, 30, 34, 38, 45, 56, 57,
70, 126; birth, 25, 26; miniature
of, 40; worthless, 129; his sister's
marriage, 128, 129; his marriage,
129–30; his debts, 129; death,
131
Clinton, The Ladies Caroline and
Henrietta Pelham-, 1, 2, 3, 4, 10,
12, 22, 32, 34, 49, 64, 120, 121
Clinton, Lady Charlotte Pelham-, 1,
2, 3, 12, 22, 32, 34, 42, 120, 121;
husband sought for, 10, 11; mode
of life, 49
Clinton, Lady Georgiana Pelham-, 1,
2, 3, 4, 10, 12, 20, 22, 32, 33–4,
42, 49, 121; husband sought for,
10, 11; receives present, 20; and
her father, 33; influenza, 35;
amazed by S, 68; on the shelf, 89;
at zoo, 121
Clinton, Lady Susan Pelham-, 54,
56, 72, 124, 127, 133; birth, 48;
misses mother, 107; at zoo,
123–4; behaviour of, 128;
courtship of, 130, 131; bridesmaid, 128; marries Lord Adolphus, 128; her extravagance, 129;
miscarriage, 131; her child, 131,
133; death, 131
Clinton, Lord Charles Pelham-, 1, 2,
4, 56; proposes marriage, 33–4;
appearance, 38; marriage, 69; and
Dolly, 130
Clinton, Lord Edward Pelham-, 1, 2,
4, 34, 38
Clinton, Lord Robert Renebald
Pelham-, 1, 2, 4, 34; blamed,
69–70, 73; accompanies L, 115;
signs father's letter, 123
Clinton, Lord Thomas Pelham-, 1, 2,
4, 34, 38; marriage, 66; effect of
Torquay, 89

Clinton, Lord William Pelham-, 1, 2,
4, 34, 36, 43; his piles, 32; love
affair with S, 1, 37–8, 134;
attaché, 48; to blame, 65; death,
124
Clumber, 1, 4, 10, 13, 22, 23, 34,
39, 42, 49, 51, 54, 55, 90, 120,
128; interior of, 3; Hamilton's
visit to, 17–18, 19, 28, 36; S ill at,
28, 36; snowbound, 34; a love
affair at, 35–6, 38, 134; Duke
dying at, 124; death of L at, 132
Como, 87, 99, 101, 107, 108, 110,
116, 119; villa at, 88, 100, 103;
Lake, 100
Corn Laws, 27, 68, 69, 89n
Cowes, 57, 58
Cowper, 7th Earl, 129
Cuddesdon, 15, 16

Damas, duc de, 7
Dent, Mrs Villiers, 33, 133
De Tabley, Lady, 48, 80n, 82–3,
84–5
De Tabley, Lord, 4, 48, 80–2
Dolly, *see* Vane-Tempest, Lord Adolphus
Douglas and Clydesdale, Marchioness of, 67, 80, 120;
courtship of, 59; appearance, 60;
rebuffs S, 73, 125
Douglas and Clydesdale, Marquess
of (later 11th Duke of Hamilton),
6, 14, 44, 46, 67, 72, 80; his
tastes, 5, 11, 12, 59; his marriage
debated, 11, 59; smallpox, 24;
betrothal, 62, 63; irked by S, 64,
73, 81, 125, 133; facilitates S's
divorce, 116; and Walpole, 120;
as Duke, 125; death, 125, 133

Egmont, Count of, 7
Erbatte, Signor, 108, 109, 111–12
Eton College, 4, 5, 15, 34, 74

Falkirk Burghs, 69
Fitzherbert, Mrs Maria, 40
Florence, 116, 118, 119, 122
Foley, Lady Emily, 89, 90
Follett, Sir William, 49, 53
Fonthill Abbey, 3, 6, 7

Gairdner, Dr, 50, 58–9, 66
Ganassini, Rev. Angelo, 109, 111
Genoa, 79, 97, 98, 100, 119
Gladstone, Mrs, 48, 54, 72, 76, 100;
    marriage, 98*n*; and L's children,
    74, 81, 105, 118, 121; belief in S,
    80, 83, 92, 116; letters to S, 79,
    81, 83, 90, 91, 95, 104–5,
    116–18; her confinement, 92, 95
Gladstone, William, 48, 53, 54, 76,
    100; character, 15; education, 4,
    15; political career, 15, 20; at
    Clumber, 35; at Rome, 47; mar-
    riage, 98*n*; his sister, 57; at Palace,
    64; his sympathy for L, 74, 96;
    and admiration, 113, 115–16;
    and L's divorce, 4, 79, 84, 108,
    113–14, 116, 122; approves
    hotels, 78, 97–8; views on pass-
    ports, 87; his Mission, 89–108;
    relationship with Manning, 92–6,
    108, 113–15, 116; writes to his
    wife, 96, 97–9, 105, 106; glimpses
    S, 106, 126; and Parkinson, 117
Gordon, Lady Margaret (wife of
    William Beckford), 6
Gordon, Sir Robert, 48
Gorham, Rev. G. C., 93
Gosford, Countess of, 85
Granville, Countess of, 7, 8
Great Britain, 65
Gretna Green, 24
Greville, Charles, 46*n*

Hafod, 3, 26, 37, 48, 67
Hahnemann, Dr, 38, 40, 41
Hamilton Palace, 8, 14, 20, 23, 59;

Lincoln visits, 5; marriage at,
    23–4; Lincolns at, 31
Hamilton, Duchess of, 13, 33, 39,
    41, 42, 44, 49, 57, 62, 63, 68, 69,
    73; girlhood and marriage, 5, 7;
    character, 7, 8, 15, 16; ill health,
    17, 32; suggests wedding presents,
    23, 59; concern for S, 18–19, 23,
    28, 37, 54, 60, 63–4, 68, 82, 84;
    to Switzerland, 45; at Wiesbaden,
    59; names guests, 60; slanders L,
    60, 83; writes to Mrs Gladstone,
    83; in despair, 120; death, 125
Hamilton, 10th Duke of (7th Duke
    of Brandon; claimed Dukedom of
    Châtelherault), 8, 10, 30, 32, 36,
    38, 42, 44, 58, 59, 61, 69, 75,
    123; description of, 5, 11, 18, 32,
    49; manhood, 5; marriage, 5–6; ill
    health, 6, 32, 121; offers S in mar-
    riage, 12, 13; in Paris, 7, 32, 39;
    financial negotiations, 17–18,
    21–2; relationship with L, 20, 28,
    31–2, 58; mediates, 27, 31; love
    for S, 12, 29, 37, 46, 55, 61, 82;
    fear of censure, 54, 55, 61–2, 67,
    74; and S's divorce, 116, 121,
    122; death, 125
Hamilton, Lady Anne, 6
Hamilton, Lady Susan, *see* Lincoln,
    Countess of
Hampden, Rev. R. D., 93
Harris, Rev. and Hon. Charles, 84
Hayter, Sir George, 31
Henderson, William, 109, 118
Herbert, Sidney (later Lord Herbert
    of Lea), 4, 74, 90
Holland, Lady, 48, 70
Holland, Lord, 48
Hope, Henrietta, 129
Hope, Henry, 129, 130
Hope, Mrs, 130

Ingoldsby Legends, The, 70*n*

Job, Ellen ('Mrs Williams'), 75, 76, 77, 81, 99, 101, 103; character, 72; appearance, 99, 111; name falsified, 87, 88, 99; packs, 77, 103, 111; flight, 106; at Verona, 108, 110; recognized, 111; refuses confrontation, 112; at Nice, 119, 120

Kingsley, Charles, 45
Kinnaird, A. F., 97, 98*n*
Koreff, Dr, 40, 46

Lamb, Sir Charles, 2nd Bt, 119, 120
Lavington, 115, 126
Leamington Spa, 18, 20, 22, 47, 69
Lecco, 107, 108
Leghorn, 86, 97
Liddell, Henry George, 4
Lincoln, Countess of (Suzie, 'Toosey'), birth, 6; character, 8, 9, 13, 15–16, 30, 76; appearance, 8, 16, 31, 51, 64, 101, 108, 112, 132; upbringing, 8–9; devotion for her parents, 8, 16, 20, 46, 58, 63, 73, 75; marriage of convenience, 12, 13, 14, 16, 24, 133; marriage settlements for, 18, 19, 20, 21–3; pregnancies 24, 32, 35, 48, 68, 86, 88, 90, 98, 104, 117; illness, 25, 31, 48, 56, 68, 77, 78, 125, and in Paris, 38–42, 44–6, 123*n*; hysteria, 19, 38; affection of the womb, 25, 31; spasms, 28, 31, 37; at Clumber, 28, 34, 54; repelled by L, 28, 29, 45, 48; love affairs, 1, 34, 35–7, 49, 55, 58, 62, 123*n*, 134; abandonment of children, 29, 51, 56, 65, 82, 105; takes laudanum, 49, 52, 54, 57, 69; prepares for separation, 51, 54, 55; her escape, 57–8; her return proposed, 60, 62; her portrait painted, 64; return of, 67–8;

at Ems, 73, 74; self-justification of, 73, 75, 85, 86, 117, 125, 133; rumours of conversion of, 76, 81; travelling impedimenta, 77, 87; adultery, 79; attracts comment, 85, 87; in Rome, 47, 84–5, 122; plans for confinement, 87, 88; falsifies name, 87, 88, 99; scandal grows, 84, 85, 90; at Como, 101–6; and Gladstone, 104, 105, 106, 117; flight, 106, 112; confinement, 108, 109, 117; takes the air, 110, 119; citation served on, 120; offers no defence, 122; changes name, 124; remarries, 124, 133; and Susan, 130, 133; death, 134; her grave, 134. At: Aix-les-Bains, 77; Baden, 73, 76; Basle, 77; Bergamo, 110; Bournemouth, 133; Brescia, 110; Cannes, 122; Civitavecchia, 84; Croydon, 133; Edinburgh, 30; Florence, 119; Frascati, 86; Geneva, 77; Genoa, 77, 88; Heidelberg, 72; Keymer, 133, 134; Lecco, 106; Leghorn, 84; Milan, 88; Naples, 48, 87; Nice, 118, 119, 131; Paris, 130, 133; Spezia, 133; Turin, 77, 83; Venice, 47; Verona, 108–12; Wiesbaden, 76
Lincoln, 12th Earl of (later 5th Duke of Newcastle), 1; upbringing and appearance, 4, 5, 13, 65; character, 4–5, 14, 29, 38, 56, 60, 69, 74, 132; and Gladstone, 4, 15, 20, 74, 92, 113, 115–16, 122; and Manning 4, 91, 93–6, 116, 126–7, 132; at Oxford, 4, 5, 14, 15, 132; political ambitions, 4, 15, 20, 23; prelude to marriage, 12, 13–14; relationship with his father, 26–7, 29, 30–1, 45, 109; relationship with S, 13–15, 19, 28, 34, 36, 39, 45, 49, 54, 55–6,

57, 60, 62, 67, 75, 91, 115, 123; marriage settlements for, 17–18, 21; marriage, 24, 134; emancipation, 26, 29; political career, 26, 35, 53, 55, 68, 129; illness, 28, 47, 66, 80, 132; and his children, 38, 49, 53, 54, 63, 65, 70, 74, 90, 123, 127, 132; sympathy for, 74, 83; expected at Como, 103, 117; divorce proceedings, 4, 69, 78–9, 110, 113, 122; his view of divorce, 115; obtains divorce, 122; effect of Peel's death, 123; becomes Duke, 124; relationship with daughter, 127–8; and Linky, 129; death, 132. Travels to: Belgium, 43; Italy, 47; Levant, 115, 122–3; Ryde, 66; Switzerland, 45; Windsor, 53, 68, 124

Liverpool, 2nd Earl of, 25, 61

London, Bedford Row, 110; Bryanston Square, 128; 14 Carlton House Terrace, 54, 55; 16 Carlton House Terrace, 90; Courtauld Institute of Art, 2n; Marylebone, 66; 59 Pall Mall, 71; 25 Park Lane, 26, 30, 32, 38, 53; Piccadilly, 130; Ponsonby Terrace, 110; 12 Portman Square, 14, 15, 26, 38, 55, 70; 17 Portman Square, 2–3, 14, 28, 128; St John's Wood, 131; Temple Bar, 109n; Wells Street, 126; Whitehall Place, 53, 54, 70

Londonderry, Marchioness of, 127–9; favours son's marriage, 128; and Susan, 131

Louis Philippe, King, 120

Lyttelton, Lady, 92, 100

Malmesbury, 3rd Earl of, 84

Mannheim, 59, 60, 63

Manning, Henry, Archdeacon (later Cardinal), 4, 90; and L, 91, 115;

126–7, 135; L's choice of, 92; faith weakened, 93–4; and the Mission, 91–6; his view of divorce, 114–15; his wife, 126n; becomes R.C., 126

Marseilles, 96, 97, 99

Melbourne, 2nd Viscount, 49n

Milan, 88, 98, 99, 107, 119

Montrose, 3rd Duke of, 89

Mount Edgcumbe, 3rd Earl of, and Countess, 85, 88

Naples, 48, 87–8, 93, 95, 99, 116; S marries at, 124, 133

Napoleon I, 6, 59; III, 125

Newark, 1, 15

Newcastle, Duchess of, 1n

Newcastle, 4th Duke of, 1–4, 34–5, 45, 65–6; character and idiosyncrasies, 1–2, 3, 124; afflicted by family concerns, 1, 33–4, 45, 48; his overtures to a marriage, 10–14; purchases, 3–4; reflections on health, 2, 10, 13, 19, 24, 25, 27, 32, 38, 40, 41–2, 48, 89; opinions of, 15, 16, 17, 26–7, 30, 33–4, 51–2, 66, 67–8, 109, 122; charmed by Duchess, 16; provoked by Hamiltons, 17, 28, 46, 54, 64; financial embarrassment, 18, 21, 47, 58, 123; to Scotland, 23–4; seeks a third title, 25; relationship with L, 26–9, 30, 47, 67–8, 122; at Ashton Hall, 27; dislike of foreigners, 30, 43, 49; and Charles's engagement, 33–4; views on popery, 48, 57; proposes marriage, 89, 90; hopes blighted, 90; illness, 120, 123; at zoo, 121; attempts a letter, 123; death, 124

Nollekens, Joseph, 3

Norfolk, 12th Duke of, 3

Northumberland, Duchess of, 68

Norton, Hon. George and Mrs, 49*n*

Nottingham, 1, 18, 43

Opdebeeck, Jean Alexis, 124, 133

Orde, Colonel James, 6, 59, 61

Orde, Madge, courtship of, 33; description of, 33–4; justifies herself, 57; at Anglesea Ville, 59, 61, 63; and S, 125

Orde, Margaret, 6, 33

Orleans, Duke of, 25

Oxford, 24, 32, 34, 132; Christ Church, 4, 5, 14; Union Debating Society, 4

Palini, 72, 75, 76, 82, 86; and luggage, 77–9

Paovich, Noele, 76, 77, 87; at Ems, 71, 72, 75; observes lovemaking, 78–9; observes S's figure, 86

Parkinson, J., 84, 87, 109, 113; and Gladstone, 116, 117, 118; imparts news, 117; examines witnesses, 121

Peel, Sir Robert, 48, 89*n*; accepts Catholic Emancipation, 26; L's affection for, 26, 123; his opinion of S, 53–4, 62; advises L, 62; sends Mission, 92, 95, 113; death, 123

Pemberton, W., 49

Potemkin, Mme, 85

Potocka, Sophia, Countess, 5

Pusey, Dr, 48

Ranby Hall, 49, 51

Ranken, Charles, 116, 117

Raphael, Lewis, 110; sees baby, 111; and S, 112, 120; and Trincavelli, 119; to England, 119; recalls Asman, 120

Reform Bill, 1, 26

Rospigliosi, Princess, 85

Ryde, 57, 66, 70, 72, 74, 109

St Leonards-on-Sea, 120

Santi, Saccomani, 87, 98, 99, 101, 103, 121; appearance, 86, 110; and Gladstone, 104, 105; prepares for departure, 106; at Verona, 108, 109, 111, 112; as godfather, 109; at Nice, 119, 120

Shaw Stewart, Lady, 75

Shelburne, Earl of, 59

Sherwood Forest, 3

Stanley, Arthur, 132

Stuart, Hon. Louisa, 59

Stuart de Rothesay, Lady, 72, 120

Sussex, Duke of, 58, 65

Swinton, James, 64

Temple, Hon. William, 87, 98

Thesiger, Sir Frederick, 92, 113

Thompson, Mr, 4, 37, 43, 72, 115

Torlonia, Prince, 88

Trincavelli, Giuseppe, 106; as valet, 101, 104, 121; collects letters, 102, 103; his orders, 102, 106, 108; and Gladstone, 105, 107; to Lecco, 107; leaves Walpole, 108; at Nice, 119

Turnor, Philip Broke, 69

Unghara, Mme, 88, 98, 99

Vane, 2nd Earl, 130, 131

Vane-Tempest, Lord Adolphus ('Dolly'), courts, 127; illness, 127, 128; behaviour, 128, 130–1; marriage, 128, 129; and Linky, 130, 131; is violent, 128, 130; to America, 131, 133; death, 131

Vane-Tempest, Lord Ernest, 128

Varenna, 103, 104, 106, 107, 108, 120

Vathek, 6

Verona, 106, 119; hotel at, 108, 110, 111

Victoria, Princess Royal, 128, 131
Victoria, Queen, 61, 68, 72, 128, 129, 131, 134; pities L, 124; takes farewell of L, 132

Waldegrave, Countess, 127
Wales, Caroline, Princess of, 6
Wales, Prince of, 53
Walpole, Horatio, birth, 109, 110; cries, 110; baptism, 109, 111; at Florence, 118; believed dead, 118, 119, 121; false report of, 132; upbringing, 132; and S, 134
Walpole, Lady, 70, 78, 80, 121, 122
Walpole, Lord (later 4th Earl of Orford), 70, 82, 83, 87, 90, 118, 122; character, 70, 78, 82–3, 103, 132; at Ems, 71, 74–5, 82; travels, 76, 84, 88, 101, 120, 122; his carriage, 72, 76, 77, 108, 120; in undress 78, 102; makes love, 78–9, 102; his behaviour in Rome, 85, 86, and at Frascati, 86;

at Como, 101–3; flight, 103–4; ill, 108, 117; at Nice, 120; at Rome, 122; and divorce, 120; death, 132
Ward, Lord, 129
Ward, Rev. (probably W. G.), 84
Welbeck Abbey, 35, 89*n*
Wellington, Duke of, at Waterloo on Copenhagen, 25
Wiesbaden, 59, 76
Wilberforce, Samuel, Archdeacon, 61, 126*n*
Wilton House, 74, 91
Winchilsea, Countess of (Emily), 38, 65
Winchilsea, Countess of (Georgiana), 28
Winchilsea, 10th Earl of, 28, 38, 65, 89
Windsor Castle, 53, 61, 68, 124, 132
Wiseman, Cardinal, 126*n*
Wolowski, Dr, 40, 44, 46
Worksop, 3